KEEPING YOUR CHILDREN SAFE

ALSO BY BETTIE B. YOUNGS

The Six Vital Ingredients of Self-Esteem and How to Develop
Them in Your Child

Self-Esteem for Professional Educators: It's Criteria #1

You and Self-Esteem: A Book for Young People

The Six Vital Ingredients of Self-Esteem and How to Develop
Them in Your Students

Managing Your Response to Stress: A Guide for Educators

Getting Back Together: How to Create a New Relationship with
Your Partner and Make It Last

Problem Solving Skills for Children

Friendship Is Forever, Isn't It?

Goal-Setting Skills for Young Adults

A Stress Management Guide for Administrators

Is Your 'Net'-Working? A Complete Guide to Building Contacts
and Career Visibility

A Stress Management Guide for Young People

Helping Your Teenager Deal with Stress: A Parent's Guide to
the Adolescent Years

Stress in Children: How to Recognize, Avoid, and Overcome It

Keeping Your Children Safe

A Practical Guide for Parents

Bettie B. Youngs

Westminster/John Knox Press
Louisville, Kentucky

The poem on page 129 ("The Paint Brush") appears by permission of Lee K. Ezell.

Unless otherwise noted, scripture quotations are from the Revised Standard Version of the Bible, copyright 1946, 1952, ©1971, 1973 by the Division of Christian Education of the National Council of the Churches of Christ in the U.S.A., and are used by permission.

Scripture quotations marked KJV are from the King James Version of the Bible.

Book design by Laura Lee

First edition

This book is printed on acid-free paper that meets the American National Standards Institute Z39.48 standard. ∞

Published by Westminster/John Knox Press
Louisville, Kentucky

PRINTED IN THE UNITED STATES OF AMERICA
9 8 7 6 5 4 3 2 1

Library of Congress Cataloging-in-Publication Data

Youngs, Bettie B.
  Keeping your children safe : a practical guide for parents /
Bettie B. Youngs. — 1st ed.
        p.   cm.
  Includes bibliographical references.
  ISBN 0-664-21976-4

  1. Parenting—United States. 2. Parent and child—United States. 3. Children's accidents—United States—Prevention. 4. Self-respect in children 5. Children—United States—Religious life.
I. Title
HQ755.8.Y68 1992
649' . 1—dc20   92-13656

To my mom and dad, Arlene and Everett Burres,
and to parents everywhere

Contents

Acknowledgments

This book has been a labor of love. It comes at a time when I am evaluating my own parenting, perhaps more than ever before. When I started to write this book I was guided by the question, "If someone else were raising my daughter, how would I want them to guide her?" That question was always in my mind. She is seventeen and a half and a first-year college student. She is facing a great number of value-laden decisions, and at a time when she must make more independent decisions than interdependent ones. I stand at a distance and watch, sometimes proudly and other times with hopeful eyes, as she puts into practice her interpretation of what I have imparted. Because of our closeness, her choices impact both of us. As she goes about asserting her will on the world, and touching lives unlike any I know, I realize more than ever that the proof is in the pudding. Yet I somehow feel she was the teacher and I the student. For that, I lovingly acknowledge my daughter, Jennifer, this young woman who is more spectacular than I could have ever imagined. I am genuinely grateful for the diligent love and nurturing she has received from her father, Dic Youngs, and from my family and friends. All adults, really, are parents to all children.

I must also acknowledge Jerry Freed at Westminster/ John Knox Press, who is responsible for bringing this book to life. I met Jerry one evening at an airline counter in Oregon among other fogged-in and weary passengers trying to return to their homes. While a number of others opted for stress tantrums, three strangers in line looked knowingly at one another and headed for the rental car counter and proceeded to drive five hours to the next airport. Sharing our work led to the inception of this book some four years later. For his commitment to the mission of his press, and for his faith in me and this work, I acknowledge Jerry, with respect and admiration. I must also thank Davis Perkins, Editorial Director, for his leadership on this project, and Katy Monk and Alexa Smith of the editorial staff and freelance copyeditor Janet Baker for their sensitive editing and contribution to this work.

I'd like to thank friend Cathy Finch and Arlene Burres, my mother, for their input and comments, and Norm Abel for his support, caretaking, and devotion throughout this project. Their contributions, as well as their inspirational energies, were very important to me.

And, last, I'd like to thank the numerous parents I've met and worked with over the years whose comments and heartfelt revelations on parenting nourished my own desire to complete this book and share it with you.

I

What Children Really Need

1

Children:
Life's Greatest Lesson

Of the many experiences in life, rearing children can be the most intense, providing not only fervent joy but occasional grave sadness. Our children cling to and reject us, adore and barely tolerate us, heal and hurt us. What we learn from these impassioned experiences leaves an indelible mark—on both parent and child.

An Exercise in Perfecting Our Own Nature

Parenting teaches some of life's most profound lessons. As we satisfy, albeit unconsciously, the unfinished business of our own unmet childhood needs, such as feelings of emotional abandonment or the longing for more hugging, kissing, and cuddling—as we strive to nurture lost self-parts or re-create the feelings of closeness, caring, and benevolence we received from our parents—the love, kindness, fairness, neglect, rage, and hurt of our own childhood pour out into our relationships with our children. In meeting the needs of these dependent people we treasure and cherish so much, our actions are often derived from the love, acceptance, and worthiness that we feel we deserve ourselves. Our parenting actions can be a reflection of our own self-esteem. Nurturing children is, perhaps, an exercise in perfecting our own nature.

If healing our hurts, mending relationships, and building more durable sand castles are among the many contributions of children, experiencing deep satisfaction, joy, and completeness and revisiting the sandbox are others.

What Have You Learned by Being a Parent?

Though we seem always to be doing for and giving to our children, we get much in return. Parenthood can be a major paradigm shift, moving us beyond our own self-centered concerns to care deeply about the needs of others. It can help us focus more clearly on the meaning of our personal journey through time and keep us from sleepwalking through life. Parenting can complete our own experience of childhood, alter our feelings of aloneness, awaken deep-seated experiences from our past, and force us to reconcile them with a new reality. The sheer need to organize and prioritize that which gives meaning or causes turmoil can cause us to live more fully than we might do otherwise. Children forever alter our consciousness.

We discover much about ourselves as we help our children learn the attitudes and develop the skills to surmount the daily challenges of life. Teaching children quite often provides parents with opportunities for learning, too. Sometimes we discover that we don't know all the answers, but for certain, we wish we did. How much have you already learned from being a parent, and how many more wonderful lessons does parenthood hold for you?

Parenting has certainly been a growth experience for me. In living with my daughter, Jennifer, in loving her, and in being her soulmate and helpmate as she learns and grows, I have learned:

Love. By loving her, I tapped into a reservoir of love and found it bottomless. I didn't know I could love so much.

Joy. As a result of my efforts, I see my daughter prosper as a healthy, intelligent, and compassionate person.

Happiness. By giving and sharing myself with her, I've experienced the deepest level of happiness. I learned that giving was more rewarding than receiving.

Empathy. In seeking to understand my child, I have put myself in her place and learned the meaning of unconditional caring. Sometimes my heart aches as I watch her struggle with a lesson or learn from a potent consequence.

Patience. Even with my guidance, Jennifer experiences the world through her own eyes, in her own time, at her own pace. You just can't hurry some things. Time, it appears, is the essence of many a lesson.

Endurance. In meeting my daughter's needs, I had to care for her when I myself was sick or had other impending responsibilities. In the face of unforeseen illness and accidents, I had to make tough decisions on my own. I learned I could. I discovered an unsuspected strength within myself.

Listening. I learned to decipher not only the various tones of Jennifer's voice but also her feelings and subtle behaviors, to hear what she was really saying rather than what I wanted her to say.

Responsibility. Because my child is so precious, I learned to accept the duties and obligations of being a parent and to be depended upon to fulfill them, even when I might prefer to be doing something else. She can count on me.

Spirituality. The miracle of her life and birth became the catalyst for renewing and deepening my own faith. Daily challenges teach me to search my heart and turn my eyes heavenward, to rest in the knowledge that I draw comfort in my faith and support from my church community.

Her needs. By listening and observing, I discovered what Jennifer needed from me and learned that sometimes it was different from what I had expected.

The fragility of human life. Though this feeling began with my pregnancy, as soon as Jennifer was born I knew her life was mine to protect, and I was committed to it at all costs. As I began to understand and value the fragility of human life, I began to take better care of my own health. Protecting her life is a compelling duty. I am often fearful. Such feelings pave the way to care about others whose lives are in jeopardy elsewhere in the world—from oppression, from hurt, from starvation, or in war. Valuing her life shaped my own work and gave me a fresh appreciation of children.

Empathy for other parents. Parenthood connects mothers and fathers everywhere. Once I sympathized with the parents of sick, crying, injured, or missing children; now I feel with them. Parenthood has made me realize that other parents have the same joys and sorrows. Sharing in this sister/brother/parenthood is very bonding. I feel closer—as though I "know" something about those who have children.

To live consciously. Because I am constantly observed by my daughter, I must be aware of what my actions convey, as well as my words. Setting a good example is an ever-present challenge. Confronting my own values up close is sometimes rewarding and at other times a bit unsettling.

To become. I surely feel I am becoming a better, wiser, and more loving person than I might otherwise have been. And, of course, I also learn what I am not but wish I were.

I've also learned:

To set priorities. After I accepted that my days were not going to get longer simply to accommodate me, I resigned myself to the fact that my desire for perfection had to go. Some things *must* be done; others are a matter of choice. People who stimulate and motivate, inspire or encourage me are important; people who drain me, are jaded or negative, or insist on seeing the cup half empty are not.

To be efficient and effective. Before I had my daughter, setbacks made me disappointed, confrontations increased my heart rate. Energy that used to be spent on tension and anxiety is now channeled into getting things done efficiently and effectively. Other people appreciate it too. They don't want people around who are stressed out, they want to be near those who perform their work effectively, with efficiency and style.

To communicate clearly and be assertive. Communicating with clarity and in sufficient detail is required in dealing with children. If children don't learn to share their toys, they won't have friends. If you let them skip breakfast, they'll be difficult and grouchy. The same is true for older kids and adults. When you're in the position of having other people depend on you—at home or at work— thinking with clarity and being consistent and assertive are essential.

To take charge. When you're in charge, you learn quickly from your mistakes and readily feel your accomplishments. I learned self-control and self-discipline.

These and other practices resulted in positive self-regard and generated high self-esteem.

The nature of adults. Basically, adults have the same needs and desires as children, though sometimes we express ourselves more subtly. I've learned that it's futile to argue or try to reason with a toddler or a teen in a tantrum. Wait until the child calms down. Children who withdraw don't really want to be alone, they mostly want acceptance and to be reassured that someone cares about them. Like children, adults behave in ways that show their needs.

Do You Enjoy Being a Parent?

If you are like me, you know that parenting is by far the most challenging and satisfying and meaningful role in life. It's also hard work. And it takes time—as much, it seems, for older children as for younger ones. When my daughter was an infant I looked forward to the time when she would be able to play independently—and when she could, she still looked around to see if I was there. When she was in grade school, her intellect was insatiable, and the need for instilling rules and guidelines for operating safely in the outer world was a must. At junior high her abundant activities required multiple bandages and a daily car pool; her questions about her feelings and her need to understand them sometimes made me feel like a clinical psychologist, with her as my entire caseload. Now that she is nearly eighteen, her need to know her place in the world and to understand the dynamics of relationships on an experiential basis occupies a good portion of her waking hours. And just as I worried when she was little that she might stick her finger in a light socket or be treated badly by another child, I'm still concerned that she might leave a burner on in the house (or an iron or hot rollers), or that she or another driver in a two-ton car will exercise poor judgment. I still want to protect her from being emotionally devastated in relationships, even though she must learn such lessons first-hand. My concerns may go on for some time. Just yesterday my own mother called and lovingly expressed her concern for my safety on an upcoming trip abroad, though I have made the same journey nearly twenty times.

Keeping Our Children Safe Today

The need to keep our children safe is an ever-present one. But how do we protect our children and keep them safe in today's world? How can we guard our children against absorbing incongruous values from harmful outside sources and protect them from dangerous activities that can change their lives in negative ways? How can we best use our parenting time to keep our children physically safe, emotionally secure, principle-centered, and motivated and curious learners? How can we best help our children to develop a sense of self that will yield inner strength and character and a rewarding and purposeful life? These are important tasks of parenting. How we do them matters.

Parenting is an awesome responsibility. Our influence is for life. My goal in this book is to help parents meet the challenge of transmitting those values and principles that can create physical, emotional, spiritual, and intellectual wellness in our children, and to do so in a way that our children may feel our loving actions and assimilate them.

It's Tougher Being a Child Today

Today's children are in need of added protection from stress, strains, and pressures, some of which their parents never imagined. Violence in the schools, drive-by shootings, crack cocaine and synthetic drugs, incessant change and a throwaway culture, dress-for-success values and personality ethics—it's a tough, more violent, and less forgiving world. In a report on the wellness of children quoted in *The San Diego Union* (July 7, 1991, p. D1), the 1991 National Commission on Children confirmed that today's children desperately need parental attention: "If we measure success not just by how well most children do but by how poorly some fare . . . children at every income level lack time, attention, and guidance from parents and other caring adults."

The small amount of quality time many parents spend with their children should be a national concern. Not spending enough focused time with children is reflected in the alarming incidence of delinquent behaviors seen today. In 1991 over a million children ran away from home. Some runaways said sarcastically their parents wouldn't even notice. Sadly, many said their parents didn't care. That was hard to believe, yet when some 34 percent of these children were located by child-find agencies who attempted to return them to their homes, many parents refused to take them back.

Not to be wanted is—both physically and emotionally— a terrible experience. The response to parental indifference is anger, and today there are many angry children, both out there and in our homes. In an age when we spend less time with our children, they need us more.

It's not just a question of finances. Money does not ensure that parents will care for their children's physical and emotional needs, spend time with them, or teach them the skills they need to grow and prosper in a healthy and functional way.

Though we say children are our future and our most precious resource, according to the statistics, our words are hollow. Many children the world over are not living in the carefree innocence we might want for them. Your children's experiences are no doubt quite different from your own. A 1989 *Newsweek* study in search of the "happy family" concluded that "the 'family' is changing. Once upon a time, families were all alike—happy. But today even the happy family isn't the same, the family just isn't what it used to be." While I'm not so sure the good old days were always so good, I do know that many families today are feeling frayed. There seem to be more dysfunctional families than ever before; both adults and children alike are searching to make sense of their lives.

The family is a good barometer of what's happening in terms of our changing social, economic, and political mores. No family is exempt from the influence of such change, and no doubt each will experience stress. This is not to say that all families are sick, but a little intensive care wouldn't hurt any of us.

We Get the Kids We Deserve

The best chance we have for raising happy, healthy, and self-confident children, and for keeping them safe in today's times, is to care for their needs and provide a positive influence by showing by example what we want for them. Kids do as we do, not as we say. You need only to hear your young daughter talk to her doll or pet to know that she parents the doll or pet exactly as she has experienced your parenting. We need to show our children that we both love and respect them, that we accept them for who they are and show them we are serious in our resolve to help them prepare to live interdependently in the world. We need to provide a solid foundation of self-esteem, set appropriate expectations, and consistently encourage and motivate our children to live purposefully. The flip side of parenting is that we must not assail them with contradictions or sabotage their formative years with actions devastating to a child's mental, emotional, physical, and spiritual growth. We must actively help our children develop the skills for building a healthy and functional life. All too often today, instead of being a strong foundation on which a child can confidently build a life, the family may be a desert of shifting sands. Some of us may have warm memories of families whose members pulled together and supported one another. This is often not the case today.

Safeguarding Children from the Dragons of Life

If being a child is harder today, so is being an effective parent. Hurried lifestyles, the belief that one's job defines one's worth as a person, and the demands of work and careers overshadowing family relationships all take their toll. Parents must contend with the disturbing influence of increased television (and music) violence and sexual exploitation, and with their children's own emotional upheavals, many brought on through their associations with other children, themselves in need of a more healthy and stable sense of self. There is the challenge of assisting our children as students—helping them derive meaning from an ever-changing and less personal school system— and the added pressure of protecting them from the

availability of alcohol and drugs. These and other new real-
ities have increased the urgency for parents to work actively to keep children safe.

What's the solution? How can we safeguard our children
from the dragons of life? While there is no simple answer,
the often-quoted words of the respected and much-admired
psychologist Virginia Satir offer a beginning: "If you can
heal the family, you can heal the world." Healthy, functional
families nurture self-esteem, buffer the stress, strains, and
pressures of daily living, offer strength and support in the
face of crisis, and provide guidance in coping with the fire-
breathing dragons lurking outside our doors.

Are You a Family or Just Living Together?

If the Waltons were around now, would they be living in
a condo, taking separate vacations, and seeing a therapist?
Today's family has been put to the test of surviving by new
family dynamics, rapidly changing social mores, and the
ever-increasing availability of stimuli outside the home—
many of which have rendered some former family interactions extinct. The high-tech information age we live in, for
example, has allowed us to lead lives that are bigger, faster,
and more colorful without necessarily bringing us closer
together. Some of us probably can remember the family
gathered at the dinner table. We laughed together, made
jokes, and maybe even took votes on which television program to watch. Now the typical American home, should
everyone even be there at the same time, is bristling with
compact-disc players, multiple televisions, telephones,
video machines, computers, and personal cassette players.
What we once watched, listened, and discussed together
we now do apart in separate rooms.

Imagine your children twenty years from now, recalling their childhood years. Will they see a loving, supportive family scene, or will the picture be one of fragmentation and chaos? Will they have warm, secure feelings, or will there be bitterness and feelings of resentment? What kind of memories of the family are you building for your children? What must you do? How much time will it take?

How Much Time Do Children Need?

Time: we're always hearing about how to make it, save it, take it, and manage it, but there never seems to be enough of it. Yet parents spending too little time with their children is one of the biggest complaints I hear from children of all ages, especially teens. That's because children equate our time with how much we love them. But is time really the issue, or do we need to examine the way we view our time, our lives, and our own nature of caring for our children? Are we *willing* to structure our lives to include enough *time* for our children? Are we *willing* to give the family priority billing? Are we *willing* to define the time we share with our children as one of the great joys of life?

Quality Time Versus Quantity Time

It's been estimated that, on average, parents of children ages four to eighteen spend less than five minutes each day in meaningful conversation with their children. Meaningful conversation is different from "Did you take out the garbage?" "Did you finish your homework?" "Did you make your bed?" or "Did you feed the dog?"

Many parents are initially surprised to find out just how important they are to their children, especially as children get older and seek the friendship of others. Yet when I ask children to list the five most meaningful people in their lives, both girls and boys name their parents as the most important. While the first person they list is their "favorite" parent ("the parent with listening heart"), the second person they name is most generally the other parent, even in cases of separation or divorce. The number-three spot goes to a favorite teacher, the teacher they consider to be the best listener, although this spot is sometimes shared by a stepparent or school custodian. The fourth person named is another teacher: this time the one whose teaching style matches the child's learning style and provides a strong base of encouragement and expectations. And in fifth place girls list their grandmothers, followed by a sibling (male or female) or anyone else who might serve as a support system; boys list an uncle, a grandfather, and then a sibling (a brother first), in that order. Peers rarely show up in the top five until children are at least fifteen.

Many parents erroneously believe their children's friends are more important to them than they themselves are. However, it's only when parents are physically or emotionally distant that children will turn to their peers for acceptance and belonging, at any cost. Not to belong is a lonely experience for anyone, most especially for children. This is when peer groups become the most influential and potentially the most dangerous. In the absence of parents, teachers, or other significant adults, most children will pay almost *any* price to belong.

The Lasting Bond: Children and Parents

At a recent seminar of mine for parents and teens, a mother and her son sat in the front row. I had been describing the parent-child bond that solidifies parents and their children. In the discussion period, this mother was the first to raise her hand.

"I don't know why John and I are always upset with each other. We used to be good friends, but now it seems like we're no longer on the same team. He seems unhappy, but he shouldn't be. He has everything, from a car—which you can bet his father and I never dreamed of having at his age—to the latest clothes and a nifty CD player. We thought these things would make him happy, but you know, when I talk with my friends, many of their kids have less but seem happier. What's the answer? What do kids want? Why can't *we* get it together? Why does my son seem so unhappy?"

I turned to John. "Do you want to take a go at that? You must have some idea. Are you unhappy?"

John shrugged. "Well, not unhappy, but just not happy: you know, *happy*. Nothing seems to matter. I don't feel very important to anyone. I'm just another kid at school; friends come and go. We aren't very close at home. I wish we were. Yeah, sure, I have a lot of *things*, but I don't have my parents. Not really. Like last week, I had a gig at school with this little band we put together. It was a big deal; you know, our first appearance. I didn't want them there for the whole thing, but you'd think they could have stopped in for a minute at the school, or maybe show up at a practice and listen to us play a little. They've never seen me perform; they always have something else to do. Two of the other four kids' folks came."

Another boy jumped in as soon as John stopped talking. "I know just what you mean. My dad and I haven't been fishing in years. When I asked him last weekend if we could go, he told me that now that I'm fifteen I should be doing those things with my friends. It made me feel as if *we* aren't friends anymore. His racquetball buddies are more important than I am!"

The answer to the old question of which is of greater value, quality time or quantity time, is: neither. It's special bonding time; it's about developing personal and emotional well-being between parent and child. It's connecting, with both parent and child feeling it.

What Do Children Really Want from You?

Have you ever wondered what children really want and need from us? I've asked the question of young people across the country. Here's what they list in order of importance.

- I want my parents to think I'm somebody special.
- I want my parents to be warm and friendly to me, just like they are to people who phone or come to the door.
- I want my parents to be concerned about me.
- I want my parents to know the "me that nobody knows."
- I want to get to talk about what's important to me and have those views be valued.
- I want to go to school with kids I relate to (children see parents as controlling this by setting up their home in a certain neighborhood).
- I want to be part of a happy family.
- I want my parents to lighten up.
- I want my parents to learn more about my feelings and emotions.
- I want to live in a world at peace (children see parents as controlling this through such acts as voting).

What is obvious about this list is its focus on internal needs, not just on getting or having things. A sixteen-year-old boy put it this way. "My dad is always telling me what he *does* for me," he said in a tone riddled with sarcasm. "I wish he'd do less *for* me and more *with* me." You can hear this in the young child who says, "Watch me, Mommy; watch, me Mommy!" or "Watch me, Daddy; watch me, Daddy!" No matter what their age, children want you to notice them. Even adult children want parental recognition from time to time. Unfortunately, too many parents become frustrated and disinterested in caretaking chores as their children get older (or even when they are very young). Some parents substitute money and things in place of time and attention. Many lose faith that they even make a difference in their child's life. Still others become easily intimidated and back off from providing the solid guidance that is needed when their children begin testing the boundaries of the very rules put in place to protect them.

Children will get our attention, one way or the other. We need to pay attention. The sad and bothersome statistics today of the numbers of young people who are destructive to themselves and others mirrors the attention they are *not* getting. Paying attention means we have to *value* our children as much as the other things we find important. It means we need parenting principles and actions that protect our children physically, emotionally, spiritually, and intellectually.

You are the most powerful force in your child's life, in every way. Genetics determines your child's physical characteristics, of course, but what you do and how you do it, your attitudes and viewpoints, will influence how your child views people, events, and the world as it is and can be. *What you do or don't do will leave an impression. How much you're there or not there will be remembered.* These interactions will serve as a framework for how your child goes about the business of living.

What Are Your Highest Values?

A common practice in helping organizations find out what they're really in the business of doing, even how to conduct business on a day-to-day basis, is to help them identify and prioritize their highest values. What exactly are your values here? we ask. We cull the list, prioritize it, and then look at the top five items. We do this because a company's mission—its work—is about its values. Priorities stem from the ranking of these values. What a company and its people should be doing is based on what they stand for. Most everything falls into place from that point on: the mission and goals of the organization, the leadership skills that are needed, the roles to be assigned, the competencies needed from the work force, and so on.

Bringing our values into focus shows us where to spend our energy and helps us to be purposeful. Like companies, parents must prioritize the many choices we have. That, more than anything else, is what being effective is all about. It's focusing on what's really important and doing it well.

As the company is shaped by its professed values, so our parenting values are reflected in our actions. Think about *your* highest values. What are they? What six areas of your life are the most important to you? What is the single most important value? Is your top priority also the most meaningful to you? Perhaps faith, family, purposeful work, friendships, health and well-being, and happiness were among your top priorities. But are you *living* your values, are you "walking your talk"? Aligning our actions with what we say is important to us isn't always easy, but it is important.

The parent-child relationship is an important, meaningful, and memorable experience. Whether you're at the stage of checking in on your newborn, still in awe as you watch your baby sleeping, patching up scraped knees, or helping with algebra homework, the next phase of your child's development is right around the corner. Don't miss your role in it. Many parents wish they had been more active in their children's childhood, wish they hadn't let so many events go unattended, or allowed so many things to happen by chance.

Parenting is central to the satisfaction or deep pain we experience in the course of our lifetime. Listen to older people reminisce about their lives, and you'll hear the same desire expressed. They never wish for a little more time to make money or express a regret at not having acquired more material objects; rather, they measure success by the great joy and satisfaction with the most precious and valuable moments of a lifetime—those spent with their children. For parents who truly experienced this challenging role in a purposeful way, it was the most joyful and rewarding time of their lives. Conversely, not giving enough attention to their children is one of the greatest sorrows expressed by those who feel they missed out.

2

How Do You Feel About Being a Parent?

In addition to establishing a mutually caring and affectionate relationship with your children, you want to keep them physically safe from harm, emotionally secure in your love, deeply believing in their worth as human beings, growing in spiritual wisdom, and intellectually stimulated so they will remain curious learners. Keeping your children safe in these ways requires a willingness on your part. You'll need a game plan. How will you manage your own life, your children's, and everything else? How will you choose what you want for them? How will you prioritize what you must do and, most importantly, accomplish all that is *worth* doing? It depends on your philosophy.

The Role of a Parenting Philosophy

A philosophy is a more or less formal statement of what you believe is worth doing. As such, it articulates what you want from your parenting role. A philosophy specifies the activities needed for keeping your children safe—for raising them in a constructive and healthy way. A philosophy defines and clarifies your actions and guides the selection of strategies for nurturing and guiding your children. It helps you to answer value-laden questions and to make decisions from among the many choices you have along the way: Should you move to a new neighborhood? Accept a new position? Stop working full time? Return to work? Change teachers for your child? Choose a better time to have another child? Postpone or proceed with a new marriage?

From my research and teaching, and in my work with parents, young people, and educators and others working with children—and from my own parenting years—I know how important it is to think about what we are doing and recognize and understand the underlying motivation of our actions—the why we do what we do—if our parenting time is to be meaningful. Parenting can be difficult, and the outcome disastrous, if we don't. At times, parenting can be frustrating, and it can easily become routine work, filled with hassles of juggling schedules and meeting the basic and important daily needs of children.

Would You Like Having You for a Parent?

There's no doubt that parenting is challenging and at times stressful, but it can also be filled with joy, meaning, and purpose. Purposeful parenting begins with having thought deeply about our intentions and plans for nurturing and guiding our children. At the heart of all parenting activity is an attitude that governs our actions toward our children and our feelings about parenthood. Each of us has a parenting philosophy already in place, and it's usually pretty obvious to others. Have you seen this one?

Susan is rushing around trying to get errands completed. She hurries toward the post office, hoping to make it before they close. Her three-year-old son is running along behind, trying to keep up. Hungry, tired, and discouraged about ever catching up to his mother, he stumbles and falls to the ground, crying. Susan yells to him to get up and, when he doesn't, dashes toward him, grabs him, and slaps him, saying, "Now you have something to cry about!" The child screams and pounds his feet on the sidewalk, refusing to cooperate.

Meanwhile, across town a similar chase is on, but with a different result.

Glenda turns to her tired and out-of-sorts three-year-old and says, "Mommy's sorry, Aaron. I'm going much too fast for you, aren't I? Here, let me carry you. We have to get to the post office before it closes. We're almost finished now, and then we can go home, fix a snack, and play." She swings him up into her arms as she dashes off in the direction of the post office. Her reassuring words, kisses, and soothing strokes comfort him. He snuggles into her arms, feeling reassured and safe. She completes her task.

You've no doubt seen similar scenes played out in a number of ways, but notice how the action toward the child differs drastically. Susan sees her son as a burden, keeping her from doing what she has to do. Her resentment and impatience win out over empathy for what it's like to be three, with short legs and not much interest in errands. Glenda's response, on the other hand, is one of empathy; she's able to understand her child's frustration and work with it in a way that's soothing to him and enables her to complete her task. Most of all, she preserves an important relationship with her child, while Susan generates bad feelings.

What is Your Parenting Philosophy?

Like Susan and Glenda, you too have some kind of philosophy in operation. So does your parenting partner. It shows up in your actions toward your children. Your parenting style reflects how you feel about being a parent. How were these decisions made? The way you were raised has a strong influence on your parenting style. Maybe you are bringing up your children the way you were raised. Possibly the opposite is true; you might be reacting *against* your parents' style, which often swings the pendulum strongly in the opposite direction. The demands of your career, your personality and disposition, your parenting partner, and your beliefs about children in general all contribute to your style of parenting. These shape your values and ideas and the decisions governing your actions. But, are they what you want?

Your actions are important: children learn what they live and live out what they learn, as Dorothy Law Nolte pointed out. Hers is a wonderful message about what children learn from our parenting.

> The child who lives with criticism learns to condemn.
> The child who lives with hostility learns to fight.
> The child who lives with ridicule learns to be shy.
> The child who lives with shame learns to feel guilty.
> The child who lives with tolerance learns to be patient.
> The child who lives with encouragement learns confidence.
> The child who lives with praise learns to appreciate.
> The child who lives with fairness learns justice.
> The child who lives with security learns to have faith.
> The child who lives with approval learns to like himself.
> The child who lives with acceptance and friendship learns
>   to find love in the world.

You Can Choose Your Philosophy

Children do learn what they live. And they generally live out what they have learned. That's a powerful reason to determine if your children are learning what you want. You're not stuck with your current actions. You can change your parenting style. You can choose what you want for your children and for yourself. You can decide what you want to bring about and create it. The first step is understanding what's going on now. Here are some key questions to get you thinking.

- What is your philosophy?
- Was it deliberately formulated, or did it just emerge?
- Is it based on what your spouse or in-laws want?
- Is it based on expectations your parents imposed on you?
- Is it based on your career demands?
- Is it based on how you were—or would like to have been—raised?
- Is it based on how your friends are raising their children?
- How is it working?
- Is it what you want?
- Are your highest values being reflected in your actions?

Translating Love and Caring Into Action

Designing a philosophy to guide your actions toward your children enables you to be satisfied and effective in your role as a parent and helps you stay in your role as protector and nurturer of your child. The following benefits of consciously choosing a philosophy of parenting are just a beginning; you will want to add your own.

- With a parenting philosophy, I understand why I do the things I do; I recognize my underlying motivation.
- With a philosophy, I can look at ideas about parenting that are reactive and influenced by my childhood and determine which values I really want to impart and which I want to change.
- I force myself to think about what is important to me, such as the love and respect of my child, and this guides my actions.
- I become more aware of my strengths, of how much I have to offer a child, how much to share, and this gives me courage and confidence to pull through the tough and challenging times.
- I set goals for myself as a parent and have a concrete objective to work toward. This helps me change what I don't like about my parenting and set new standards to achieve.
- I become more clear about what I really want for my children and what I'm actually giving each one.
- I become more aware of my own repressed but natural resentments about parenting, such as the lack of freedom and the sacrifices, and am able to acknowledge these in a healthy manner.

Designing Your Parenting Philosophy

How do you decide what you want for your children? Start by writing down your ideals—those things you would like to bring about in your parenting. Do this for *each* of your children. Call it your THIS I BELIEVE paper. This serves as a way to brainstorm all you truly believe and would like to aspire to in your parenting role. I'll share the original working paper I did for my daughter with you. This was designed years ago, when I first began a serious quest for the beliefs I held about parenting and hoped to put into practice as I went about my life. This paper then gave way to a second and third draft, each one further clarifying not only my intentions but my actual involvement in my child's life. I've used the first draft here rather than the re- fined copies that followed, in order to give you an idea of how to begin.

- I have but one year to see my daughter be 1, 2, 3, 4, 5, 6, 7, 8, 9, 10, 11, 12, 13, 14, 15, 16, 17, 18 (and so on). I very much want to know her at each of these ages.
- I want so much for her to respect, love, and really care about *me*. I want to do the right things in bring- ing about these conditions.
- I don't have all the answers to parenting my daugh- ter. Her needs keep changing. Though my parents showed me what love and caring were about, I need to keep observing her, watching her needs in keep- ing her safe, talking to others about what they have learned, and reading. Because she is so important to me, I don't want to ever say "I wish I had . . ." but rather "I am . . ."
- I want always to ask, "How's my daughter faring: at home, at school, with friends, with me?"
- I want her to experience me and my love and caring. I want us to form a special and rich relationship togeth- er. I want our bonding to last all my lifetime and hers. I will take the time to create and sustain our relationship.

- I will examine the effects of my lifestyle on her and change it if it means protecting and preserving her well-being.
- I want her to be happy, to know an inner joy. I will encourage her to embrace a spiritual consciousness.
- I want her to be healthy. I will emphasize nutrition. I will care for her when she is ill and be responsible about her health care.
- Remembering the pride I felt when my mother would come to school to pick me up, in thinking she was the most beautiful woman I knew, I'd like my daughter to feel proud of me. I will stay fit and in good health for me and for her, that I may exemplify the importance of fitness and health and feminine beauty.
- I promise to keep her safe. I will not harm her physically. I will not allow others to harm her. I will see that she is always in an environment that values safety.
- I will strive to place her in surroundings where others value their children's emotional health as I do hers.
- I will foster her self-esteem; I will not belittle her or swear at her. I will not be emotionally abusive to her. I will help her believe in herself and develop a healthy sense of respect for others.
- I will strive to develop her talents and interests by exposing her to activities that she's interested in. I will try not to impose my interests on her solely for my own reasons but, rather, to sense what she's about—to help her define her mission and purpose in life.
- I will help her learn self-control and self-discipline.
- I will always present her father in a positive light, as the loving and caring father he is. I will foster a life-long friendship with her father so that she, too, may have him as her best friend.

- I want her to know my parents and the richness of their love, talents, and interests, as well as other family members—my brothers and sisters and their children. I will work toward keeping those bonds connected, no matter where I may choose to live in the world.

- I will postpone certain elements of my career development if need be, especially in her early and teen years, in order to keep her safe and emotionally well. I will evaluate my work roles to see if they are having a seriously adverse effect on her or our relationship. I will design my work around what is productive and of value to me and share the joy of purposeful work with her, so she will come to know the joy of productive work as a value for her.

Do your paper now. Don't put it off or say you'll do it later. It doesn't matter how old your children are; they needn't be infants for you to begin. Encourage your parenting partner to do this exercise too.

After you've completed your THIS I BELIEVE working paper, you're ready to sum it up into a philosophy statement. The first draft of my statement looked like this:

- I love and value my daughter; I will be an active and nourishing part of her life.
- I will protect her from physical harm and emotional hurt and will strive to keep my lifestyle, work, and health in harmony with my needs and hers.
- I hold her as a priority in my life; she will be an important factor in the decisions I make.

When you complete your philosophy statement, frame it and put it on your desk beside the projects that have a tendency to consume your life. Put a copy on the bathroom sink or where you get dressed each morning to remind yourself how important it is to use your parenting energies wisely. After all, childhood is very brief. Make your parenting years count.

What Are Your Family's Core Values?

Just as each parent has a philosophy that serves as a guide for parenting actions, healthy families have a central core of articulated and felt values. A healthy functioning family pulls together, understanding the necessity for unity, even though individual members have needs and goals of their own. This accepted mission becomes the constitution that governs family life. Though it may not be written, there's one operating in your family, exerting influence on what goes on there. To examine the one currently in existence, try writing out a description of what is currently happening—the mode of operation—in your family. Then examine it. Imagine how the following mission statement would govern your actions and the actions of each family member: "In our family, each person is valued. Each person has a right to be listened to and shown respect. All persons have a responsibility to themselves, to one another, and to the family unit."

What Is Your Family's Mission?

What is your family mission statement, and how does it govern family life? Is it what you want? If not, you can change it. If it needs changing, chances are that other family members will welcome the change too.

Writing a mission statement takes deep introspection. Reviewing it forces you to think through your priorities and to align your behavior with your beliefs, so you're not being driven by everything that happens to you but, rather, by what you're trying to do. A mission statement is an important way to help you and your parenting partner to examine your individual parenting philosophies, and see how they are similar and different, as well as how they complement or detract from each other. Take the time to write out what you want for your family, and then have your family do it together. You'll find it will be a heart-warming exercise, one in which all members get a chance to understand more fully their roles and places in the bosom and safety of the family.

The capacity to enjoy our families seems to come more easily to some than to others. Sometimes parents have a difficult time learning to leave a messy desk at work or a kitchen in disarray in order to relax and play with each other or with their children. They feel a moral obligation to be a good provider or a perfect housekeeper that precludes their closing the door on disorder and going for a walk in the park or around the block together. Yet time taken to play and relax pays off in ways clean desks and clean floors never can. Neither our mates nor our children will ever again be as they are now. If we don't take the time now to enjoy them, we've lost an opportunity forever. Healthy families know this, and time together is given high priority. Think carefully about what you want for your children and what you want from your parenting experience.

II

*Keeping Your Children
Safe Physically*

3

Are Your Children Safe at Home?

"As a parent of two young children," said Cathy, "my greatest daily concern for them is that they feel safe and loved. I want them to feel that their home is a place they belong and are wanted. My children spend so much time away in ever-changing and sometimes challenging environments that's it's even more important to me that our home conjure up feelings of love and safety to them."

Picture yourself as a small child, running from a thunderstorm, frightened and anxious. Or perhaps you're hiding from the neighborhood bully, who has a squirt gun with your name on it. Maybe you skinned your knee and need a big hug. In each case, where do you turn?

Home. A refuge, a haven, a place of warmth and love and acceptance. In his book *Homing in the Presence,* Gerhard Frost says:*

> Observe the traffic of children if you would know the meaning of home. In every mood they turn toward home.

---

*Here and throughout, publication facts not given in the text may be found in the list of Suggested Readings at the back of the book.

Whatever their need of the moment, they are great homers. Sometimes with a tear on each cheek; sometimes with a secret too good to keep; sometimes with a question that won't wait, sometimes just hungry, or tired or guilty—always the child turns toward home. The door is the child's symbol of home, and hope.

Even when we get older we still go home, if only in our memories.

As parents we want our children to think of home as a place where they will be secure . . . and safe. Keeping our children physically safe means we protect them from harm: in our homes, schools, and neighborhoods. It also means we care for their health by providing good nutrition, adequate rest, and exercise and guard them from the harmful effects of stress overload. It means we seek medical attention and dental care when they need it and safeguard them from becoming victims of chemical and substance abuse. All children have a right to such safety, yet we live in a world where many children are subject to sexual abuse, physical assault, starvation, homelessness, inadequate health care, and neglect. That so many of our children should fall victim to these conditions is not only embarrassing but wrong.

Do your children think of home as a place where they are assured of their safety? Is it a nourishing haven to come home to?

Home Is a Feeling as Much as a Place

Your children must see home as a nonthreatening environment. That means they must feel safe *with* their parents (and others who live there) and feel safe *in* the building. Finding out how safe your children feel is important to you, because without a feeling of safety, your children become victims to fear. Would you stay in a job if you were afraid there? Would you shop at a center where you were afraid to walk to your car unaccompanied? Probably not.

You might be surprised to learn how your children feel about safety at home. Take the time to evaluate their sense of safety—through their eyes. Ask yourself and your children the questions shown below. Children's responses often differ from their parents', so listen closely. Be sensitive to what they say. Your children's perception—real or imagined—can help you find ways to best ensure their safety.

- Do my children feel we live in a safe neighborhood? Why? Why not?
- Are there neighbors my children feel comfortable about asking for help if I'm not here?
- How safe is my home?
- Are there places in our home that are frightening to my children?
- How much time do my children spend alone at home?
- Do they know what to do, whom to call, where to go in case of an emergency, if I am not there? Have we discussed (for small children) using the telephone? Is it within reach?
- Do my children feel that family members are non-threatening, encouraging, and positive people?
- Do they seem comfortable to stay home with siblings or the other parent, or are they really upset when I'm not around?
- Do my children show fear of anyone associated with our home—parents, siblings, relatives, or service people?
- Are my children proud to bring friends home, showing off the house and especially their rooms?

- Do my children (especially teenagers) feel this is "my home," not just "my parents' home?"
- Do they fear being alone?
- What is my philosophy of discipline? Is it fair or harsh—do I strike, hit, swear?
- Who disciplines my children besides me? What is that person's approach to discipline?
- Are my children afraid of *me*?
- What *are* my children's fears?

Discipline is About Setting Safe Boundaries

All of us are afraid to be hurt by someone who is bigger and more powerful than we are. And that's what punishment represents to children. Discipline is about teaching children that there are consequences for not keeping within the boundaries of established rules, not about being hurt. When your children misbehave, do you react based on how you're feeling at the moment, or do you have fair and appropriate consequences for inappropriate behavior?

As children go about growing and changing and learning in each new phase of childhood, they must surmount many challenges along the way. Through trial and error they explore what works and what doesn't. Children are more in need of models than critics. When you clearly articulate your expectations, your children can better understand what is required of them; when you illustrate the behavior you want them to embrace, they are more likely to emulate it. When you clearly delineate the boundaries and spell out consequences when these boundaries are violated, children learn to monitor their actions and become responsible for the actions *they have chosen.*

Consequences involve follow-up, making sure a child understands the reasons for going in a certain direction and then follows that path. I call this guidance; some call it discipline. Either way, shaping a course of direction you want your children to follow begins with making sure that *you* know what you want your child to learn and are then willing to show them.

Faye told me about the difficulties she was having with her two sons, twelve-year-old Jimmy and fifteen-year-old Justin. It seemed to Faye she was continually called upon to intervene: to determine who was right or wrong, whose music would be played on the CD player, who got to use the telephone and for how long. "All I do is play referee for my sons," she complained. "It's not fun, and I always end up as the ogre for one of them. The worst part is, I don't seem to be making a difference. The same old problem emerges again and again, no matter how much I yell and scream. The boys just go right back to the same thing the next day."

I encouraged Faye to see how she was exemplifying the old saying, "Do as I say, not as I do." She was telling her sons not to yell and lose their tempers, even as she was yelling and losing hers. She was telling them to solve a problem once, yet allowing herself to be dragged back into the same old problem over and over again. She wasn't modeling the behavior she wanted them to follow.

Knowing how difficult it would be to keep her temper with her sons when they were yelling, Faye wrote out a small card for herself and kept it handy. The card read, *These are only boys, even if they sometimes look like men. They want and need my guidance. They will follow it only if they respect the one giving it—me. They will respect it only if they can see me following it. I will be calm, listen to both sides equally, make a decision, and stick to it. I will refuse to be drawn into the same argument. I will stay focused on teaching them to learn to resolve problems in a win-win fashion, one that works for both of them.*

Although Faye would backslide at times, she tried to maintain her new approach. As she did, she saw a remarkable change in her sons' behavior. The last time we spoke, she was full of enthusiasm. "Parenting is more satisfying now. It's also a lot more fun. There are still problems, but they're new ones. My sons are learning new skills that help them address new areas. They've learned how to communicate with other and are quickly learning how to confront each new issue and resolve it, sometimes without me. Now I feel more like a teacher than a referee, and I sense that the boys respect me much more, which makes me feel better about myself."

Imitating is the way most of us learn. No matter how many times you say, "That's different; I'm an adult," or "Do as I say, not as I do," your children are going to act from what they see and hear. If you tell your son not to lie, but then have him lie on your behalf, such as, "If that's Mrs. Peterson, tell her I'm not home now!" you send out a contradiction, and he'll lie too. You might quit smoking so your child never begins. That's positive modeling. Remember, our values always show up in our actions.

How Are You Managing You?

When Faye changed her approach from disciplining to teaching, she saw progress in her sons' behavior. Do you discipline on the basis of crises, moods, quick fixes, and instant gratification? Or, are your actions centered on the values you want to instill in your children? You may want to review the list of values you identified in chapter 1 to determine whether these values are being expressed and reinforced in your parenting actions. You'll get a better sense by writing out your responses to the questions below. Doing so allows you to examine carefully what's going on now and can give expression to the values you want to bring about for your children. The point of this exercise is to help you focus on what you're trying to do, rather than simply responding to or being driven by a momentary crisis.

- What am I trying to teach my children by my approach to disciplining them?
- What do I want them to learn?
- Do I admire my style of guidance and direction?
- Would I like to be governed by this approach?
- How are my children faring under my guidance?
- Is my approach working? Am I getting the positive results I want?
- Is my style of guidance and direction consistent with my values?

Great Kids Misbehave Too!

Parents and their children are generally at least twenty years apart in age, experience, and reasoning ability. They also have different ideas, expectations, beliefs, and values about themselves, one another, and what they want. For example, children are not born knowing that it isn't all right to write on walls and will learn to express their artistic talents on the appropriate medium only if their parents consistently teach them *where* they can write. Children do not see their tantrums as a problem; they simply have not yet learned more appropriate or self-controlled ways to channel their frustrations and to vent their emotions.

Are you aware of your own tolerance for teaching your children appropriate ways to respond? Do you separate the actions from the behavior when you correct your children's behavioral faux pas? Calling your son lazy because he doesn't make his bed or pick up after himself will do little to get him to make his bed or pick up after himself. About the only effect it will have on him may be to contribute to an unhealthy self-image and possibly become a self-fulfilling prophecy.

Concentrate on constructive ways of changing behavior, such as explaining specifically what to do and how to do it and then assisting your children with those tasks until they understand the standards for them. In their excellent book *Discipline Without Shouting or Spanking*, authors Barbara Unell and Jerry Wyckoff provide a summary of effective disciplined parenting. These principles are based on over twenty years of behavioral research, proving that it's important for practical as well as philosophical reasons to separate the child from the behavior when you deal with misbehavior problems. Here are their recommendations:

Decide on the specific behavior you would like to change. If you deal in specifics rather than abstracts, you will manage better.

Tell your children exactly what you want them to do and show them how to do it. If you want your son to stop whining when he wants something, tell him how to ask you. "Jason, when you want a glass of milk, say, 'Mommy, may I have more milk?'" If you want Jason to make the bed in a certain way, show him step by step and then make a point of coming into his room for several days (or longer) to help get it right.

Praise your child's behavior. Don't praise the child; focus your praise on behavior, because that is what you are interested in controlling. "It's good you're sitting quietly" rather than "You are good for sitting quietly."

Continue the praise as long as the new behavior needs that support. Praising all the correct things that your children do reminds them of your expectations and continues to hold your own model of good behavior before them.

Try to avoid power struggles. Using a "beat-the-clock" technique when you want your children to get ready for bed faster, for example, will help you reduce parent-child conflict because you transfer the authority to a neutral figure, the kitchen timer.

Supervise. Children need fairly constant supervision. If you are there while they are playing, you can help them learn good play habits; if you're around while homework is being done, you can monitor study habits.

Avoid being a historian. What is done is done. Working toward a better future makes more sense than dwelling on history. Reminding children of the errors they make only gives them examples of what *not* to do; it doesn't show them what to do. If reminding children about their errors does anything, it acts as practice in making errors.

Teach Children That All Actions Have Consequences

There's a consequence for everything. The consequence of eating too fast is a stomachache. The consequence of doing a good deed is positive feelings. The consequence of going out in the cold with wet hair is a head cold. The consequence of staying up too late watching TV is being tired and sluggish the next day. It's important that children understand cause and effect and realize that, while they can't control the consequences, they are in charge of the actions leading to those consequences.

In Brad's home, the consequence for not getting to school on time is having his car privileges revoked and being taken to and from school by his father the next day. Sally has a rule that toys that remain on the floor for two days go into a special barrel; her children may not play with them for a week. Structuring a consequence is part of the leadership of parenting. However, it is important that consequences be related to the event and reasonable (it makes perfect sense to take a toy away for a week if it is not put away; it makes no sense to small children to put them to bed an hour early because their toys are on the floor).

Consequences should be fair, in proportion to the offense, and without recrimination. Children should always see the possibility and the necessity of making a fresh start. Decide on reasonable, clear rules and enforce them consistently. Make only those rules that you believe to be truly important, to which your child can adhere, and that you intend to enforce. If your child breaks a rule, the consequences should be certain, prompt, and related directly to the offense. Seventeen-year-old Derek and his best friend left school at lunch in his car. Lunch took longer than they planned, and since they were late anyway, they decided they wouldn't go back to class. The school, alarmed at their absence, called their parents. When Derek came home, his mother, without threatening, name-calling, or dramatics ("Do you know what your life would be like if you didn't get your high school diploma?"), fit the punishment to the crime. What she did say was, "Derek, we agreed when you got the car that you would use it in a responsible manner. Driving off campus without permission and cutting classes and driving around all afternoon is not responsible. I'll take you to school and pick you up after school for the next week. At the end of the week, if you feel you can behave responsibly again, your driving privileges will be restored."

For the next week, his mother drove Derek to school. You might argue that her response was a hardship on her too. That's often the case, but it pays off in the long run. Your children need to know that you are serious in your resolve to help them learn appropriate behavior. Derek didn't cut school again.

Punishment has impact because of its certainty, not because of its severity. Always discuss the consequences in advance with your children. Let them know the cause and effect of their punishments. They need to understand that they are responsible for their actions. A consequence is not something you "do to them"; it is the direct result of their actions. You must be consistent. If you said the keys would be taken away for breaking curfew, take them away each time. Children need continuity of guidance. And finally, be sure the consequence comes close on the heels of the action, especially for very young children. Children go on to other things very quickly. They will not learn the lessons you are trying to teach them about responsibility if they break your rules on Monday and are punished on Friday.

When children learn to experience the consequences of their acts, it teaches them to be responsible for what they do. Responsibility builds self-esteem because it gives them control. They are not attacked or berated, and they don't have to feel guilty; their relationship with you is not on the line. You still love them and care about them even though they made a mistake.

Good Actions Have Consequences Too

It's easy to get caught up in the responsibilities of disciplining for negative behaviors and forget to give praise for good actions. In a day full of "Don't touch that!" and "What were you thinking when you . . . !" and more than one "Don't do that to your brother!" we tend to overlook the good behavior we see. Children need to see both sides of the results of their behavior. Just as ignoring rules and misbehaving have consequences, being good and behaving well have consequences. Just as you did with bad behavior, emphasize specifically what good behavior brought about the consequence. "Jordan, you did a very good job of cleaning up the bathtub after your bath this evening." And, also as you did with bad behavior, make the praise commensurate with the deed.

Sexual Abuse Is Cruel and Inexcusable

Being sexually victimized is tragic. Coupled with physical pain is emotional anguish, both taking an enormous toll on the value children place on their worth. Youngsters who fall victim to sexual abuse suffer physical hurt and psychic pain that can last a lifetime. It can also result in their hurting others. Research shows that sexually abused victims often repeat the cycle with their own children.

If you are sexually involved with your child, get help immediately for coming to terms with it. There are community centers to help you learn how to overcome these destructive actions toward your child and discover healthy ways to care for yourself. If your parenting partner is molesting a child and you're afraid to do something for fear of retaliation, get assistance. Call your local information hotline for service agencies in your community. Many of these are offered without cost to you. Make an appointment with a child, family, or marriage therapist in your community to talk about what you can do to change the situation. The How to Find Help section at the back of this book lists some references and support services as one way of beginning. Another is to call the counseling services located at the central administrative center in your local school district and ask them for sources of assistance to parents and their children (many of these services are provided at minimal or no cost).

Make your home a secure, comforting and nurturing place in which your children feel safe and cherished. A loving environment for your children throughout their growing years not only keeps them safe and healthy but is the blueprint they'll use to nurture their own families. Feel comfortable about reaching out for help during a crisis. If you're going through a trauma such as separation, divorce, job change, or personal chaos and worry about the effects on your children, get assistance. You may want to become part of a support group. Getting help to learn a positive approach to dealing with your children while your resilience is low is a sign of health, increases your self-esteem, and assists your children in getting through tough times without suffering long-term consequences.

4

Can Your Children Take Care of Their Bodies?

It's easy to think about physical safety in "outside" terms: that is, the environment. While having safe homes, neighborhoods, and schools is vital, there is one environment in which your children are going to spend more time than any other: their own bodies. Have you taught your children the importance of safeguarding their bodies? Have you instilled the value of wellness? Do they know that the responsibility for one's health is a personal one? Have you taught them about the body's need for a proper diet and good nutrition? Are they learning these messages based not only on your words but also by what they see you do—by what occurs in their home? Have you taught your children about the body's need for adequate exercise and relaxation? Again, are they learning by your actions to make these habits a part of their lives? Do they know how to manage stress and draw vitality from it?

The Importance of Diet and Nutrition

Your children's nutrition not only fuels their bodies and energy levels for the day but contributes to their overall health and wellness. To a great extent, as health experts say, "We are what we eat." Good health depends on a balanced diet. A deficiency of certain vitamins, minerals, and nutrients can upset body chemistry. An unbalanced diet, or any diet that emphasizes one type of food (proteins, fats, carbohydrates) to the exclusion of others may be very harmful to the body, especially when stress, illness, and injury are superimposed. The body that is depleted of essential nutrients is even less capable of withstanding the ravages of stress and strains of life, making it even more susceptible to major health breakdowns.

Can you list what your children had to eat today? What did they have for dinner yesterday? When was the last time they had proteins, carbohydrates, and a full complement of vitamins and minerals all in one meal? You may not be aware of your children's eating habits (only of the fact that whatever you bring home from the store disappears with alarming speed) but you should be. Just as good diet and nutrition play a vital role in your well-being, they play an even greater role in the developmental years.

Teach Your Children About Nutrition

Teaching the importance of good nutrition starts early, but making sure it carries over into the teenage years is especially important. All children need three meals a day, with an emphasis on dark green and yellow vegetables, whole grain or enriched cereals and breads, and milk. Active children and those engaged in strenuous physical activities also need snacks rich in protein, minerals, and vitamins. When a child's body lacks essential nutrients, it simply cannot function properly. School performance is naturally affected because skipped meals (and nutrients) can make a child tired and less able to cope. Research links the omission of breakfast as a major factor in a youngster's inability to function in school. Children who have breakfast and lunch show significant improvements in hemoglobin concentrations, resulting in overall better school performance on tasks demanding attentiveness and alertness. It's estimated that nearly 70 percent of all school-age children come to school without breakfast; more than 30 percent of adolescents who skip breakfast also skip lunch. It's not always easy to improve our children's dietary habits, but the following suggestions can help.

Breakfast is a must. Breakfast should not be missed (by either adults or children), and ideally should consist of fruits and grains that will steadily release glucose during the day, giving fuel to the brain. All too often, children tend to rush off to school with breakfast in hand, if they get any at all. Planning the night before can help to make breakfast time a little easier. If the table is set with plates, bowls, glasses, and silverware so that children have only to pour juice in a glass and pop the bread in the toaster, they will be more likely to eat something nutritious. If the entire family can rise early enough to eat together, even better! If breakfast is on the table, most likely your children will eat it. It does take some planning on your part to get everything ready the evening before, but it's well worth it.

Make family mealtime a cooperative effort. Good nutrition needn't be all your responsibility. Children can take turns being responsible for meals. Or meal preparation can be a cooperative effort. Plan menus on weekends so that all the needed food items will be on hand. You can even go so far as to write a weekly menu, allowing each parent and child to plan favorite meals. Other variations can be one adult and one child jointly share the responsibility and plan special meals. However your family chooses to do it, meal planning and preparation can be fun, when family members are involved, and makes healthy eating a learned habit.

Avoid conflict at meals. It's difficult for the body to digest food when the mind is in turmoil. By carrying on pleasant conversations, meal time becomes a part of the day to which each member looks forward. Make it a time to share the positive events of the day and to exchange feelings of goodwill. This is not a time to resolve family conflicts: don't allow heated discussions to be carried out. Make fun, laughter, peace, and tranquillity the norm.

Beware of special diets. Your "body-building" or "on-the-team" son may have special needs, to the exclusion of a balanced diet. If he is on the school wrestling team, he may be trying to drop weight (to compete in a lower weight class). He may go on a binge-and-purge diet. Wrestlers, for example, eat little or nothing for three or four days before a match, and then immediately after the wrestling match go on a food binge to make up for days of near starvation. Do get expert medical advice before permitting your child to go on any diet that is not completely balanced in all areas. Calling on medical experts to give advice can often help you persuade your athlete to do sensible nutritional planning.

When teenage girls diet they generally focus on losing weight for appearance reasons. Ever concerned about their growing and changing selves, many teenage girls are very self-conscious about being overweight. Ranging from fad diets to the extremes of binge-and-purge diets, the incidence of eating disorders like anorexia and bulimia is highest in adolescent girls, as is the use of diet pills. If you notice any drastic change in your daughter's eating habits, from excessive consumption to merely picking at her food, don't let it go unmentioned. Talk about it with her to see if she can pinpoint what's going on. Causes can range from a simple momentary episode of stress, to one she needs help in resolving, to a psychological or medical problem that needs expert attention. If you notice a change that lasts longer than a few days, take action. Ask your family physician to assess your daughter's state of health and suggest the best way to meet her nutritional needs, especially when dieting.

Don't contribute to a weight problem. Just as dieting can be harmful if not done carefully, being overweight poses problems too. You can unknowingly be contributing to poor eating habits and weight problems in your children. Are foods, especially sweets, being used as a reward? Are you fixing too many easy dishes containing mostly starches? Have your children learned to turn to food for self-gratification or do they eat as an outlet for depression? Look for patterns in food consumption. When do your children snack? What are their favorite fattening foods? Do they overeat when feeling blue or bored or propped in front of a favorite television show? Observe the meals you prepare; if you feel they are nutritious but your child is overweight, you may wish to consult your family physician, school nurse, or nutritionist for ways to help your child deal with his or her weight problem.

The Importance of Fitness and Exercise

We often assume that our children get sufficient physical activity when this may not be true. Children's lives are more sedentary than we might think. Even in the schools, children are getting fewer and fewer opportunities to get and stay fit. In some school districts across the nation, physical education classes—which used to be mandatory throughout high school—are now elective in a student's final years. Often a student will waive the opportunity to take physical education in order to participate in another textbook education health course. It's not much better at the elementary level. Current recommendations are that compulsory school physical education programs be instituted for fifty minutes each week. Too often this fifty minutes is scheduled into one class period once a week, usually the last period of the day, so the school doesn't have to contend with children taking showers, with the resulting towel expense and water use.

The executive director of the President's Council on Physical Fitness and Sports, Ash Hayes, warned in "Family Fitness," a *Reader's Digest* special report, that "millions of Americans in every age group are unfit. One important solution to this shocking national problem is for parents to accept responsibility for their own physical fitness and for that of their children. Working together in family activities in a spirit of fun and cooperation is one of the very best hopes we have of getting ourselves in shape."

How to Help Your Children Be Fit

Ensuring that your children are fit and healthy has to do with how much exercise they are getting. There are a number of benefits derived from exercise. Exercise can:

- Strengthen muscles, bones, and ligaments
- Increase blood circulation
- Contribute to a healthy heart

- Increase resistance to disease
- Add oxygen to the body
- Sharpen mental acuity
- Relax nerves, and balance emotions
- Reduce fatigue
- Improve figure and complexion
- Aid digestion

You can take an active role in helping your children get the exercise they need. Here's how.

Set an example. As parents, we need to be positive role models for our youngsters. If you smoke a pack of cigarettes a day, and sit in front of the TV eating potato chips when you return from work, your child will most certainly not learn how to become physically fit. If you want to have credibility with your child, get involved in some type of fitness program. If you aren't fit, work toward it; if you are fit, stay fit. You want your child to see the importance of fitness to overall health. Again, your child is setting patterns to take along into adult life. You are the model for what that will be.

Encourage individual activities. See to it that your children are involved in activities that channel their need for risk, adventure, and challenge in a productive and positive way. Don't depend on the school to do this, and don't assume that it is the school's responsibility (or anyone else's) to keep your children fit. Encourage sports such as bicycling, swimming, skiing, surfing, horseback riding, and other activities that incorporate and combine a high degree of physical and mental coordination.

Encourage team sports. Have you ever watched children during swim team practice? Undoubtedly they get as much exercise horsing around with their friends as they do from the formal practice. The same is true during soft-ball practices, soccer games, and other team sport activities. Additionally, interacting with others allows a child to do a lot of laughing and shouting, releasing aggression and lessening stress. It would be a little odd for a child to jog alone, yelling out loud; doing so during team practice is encouraged and is a great way to blow off steam.

Develop family fitness. When your children were little, you probably loved going on family outings, taking walks during Indian summer evenings, bicycling to the park, swimming at the lake. As your children became teenagers, they probably pulled away from such family activities, preferring to spend more time on their own. If you feel that a child needs to work on fitness, perhaps it's time to start up the family sports unit again.

Saturdays and Sundays are a good time for family outings. Going to the beach, camping, hiking, and bicycling are loved by all and with a little planning can be a regular part of your family's time together. Family activities should include physical fitness routines; working together in the spirit of fun and cooperation is one way to make fitness a total part of our health routine. "Family Fitness," the Reader's Digest special report, suggests four specific ways to get your family involved in physical fitness. They are:

1. Sign contracts. Have each family member write down one fitness goal for the month. For example, "I want to be able to run one mile nonstop." Sign and date the contract and have it co-signed by a family member.

2. Exercise as a family. Agree to exercise one half hour before watching TV, or just before dinner. If schedules are too complicated during the week, set a time

on Saturday and Sunday. Then everyone can exercise independently during the week.

3. Record scores. Post a chart on the refrigerator for the scores of each family member. Update the chart each time you retake the test and record each workout.

4. Reward achievements. When you reach a goal, give yourself a prize (fitness clothing or sports equipment, not food). When all family members reach certain goals, reward everyone with an activity you all enjoy—and participate as a family. For example, you might take a fitness vacation (such as backpacking) together.

Build fitness slowly and regularly. The essential component of any effective health program is that it be aerobic in nature (one in which you have to breathe heavily but don't consume oxygen faster than your heart and lungs can supply it). Experts recommend three 20–30-minute sessions of vigorous activity weekly. These can include walking, swimming, bicycling, aerobics, Jazzercise, etc. Remember to start your child (and yourself!) slowly if you are not in shape. Again, consult your physician if your child is overweight or has any health problems, or if you are in doubt about your child's health.

Your Children's Checkups

Other important health care needs include your children's regular medical and dental checkups. Starting in infancy, it's important to see that they get immunization shots, eyesight checkups, and, periodically, a medical examination to ensure that they are growing and developing normally. Your children's pediatrician can help you stay abreast of their health. And don't forget, teenagers need medical checkups too. Watch closely that your children are in good health, and teach them that good health isn't an accident; keeping the body fit and healthy is a deliberate and responsible parenting action.

The Importance of Relaxation

Another key to feeling safe inside one's own body is being able to produce a relaxation response when needed or wanted. Adults too often think that children have no trouble relaxing. We see our small ones sound asleep, looking like angels without a care in the world, and assume all is well. We tend not to realize just how stressful a child's life can be. But what about the toddler who screams in a tantrum because he can't get his message across due to underdeveloped verbal skills? What about the twelve-year-old girl seated this year next to a boy still in his "I'd rather eat worms than sit next to a girl" stage? What about the teenager who fears the whole world will think he is a nerd because his ogres of parents won't give him a car when all his friends have vehicles? What about the captain of the hockey team, already nervous about her performance in tomorrow's game? Like adults, children experience stress and need to learn to relax.

Teaching Your Children to Relax

As adults, we all have ways of relaxing. One person might play a round of golf, while a second takes a hot bath. What works for one person may not be considered relaxation for another. The same thing is true for children. Teach your children the importance of relaxation to the body's wellness, and then help them learn some basic relaxation skills.

Fourteen-year-old Benjamin sometimes gets excruciating headaches. When this happens at home, he goes to his room, puts on a relaxing tape and lies down. He pictures himself flying a plane (his goal is to be a pilot someday) over the ocean. The sound of the engines is a soothing drone, and Ben hums along. He pictures the ocean as vivid blue in some parts, aqua in others, and almost green in yet others. He rolls back and forth on his bed, imitating the gently rocking motion of the plane as he takes it across the Pacific, seeing small islands below him. He is in control. No one is in the plane but him. He can go wherever he wants. After fifteen minutes, Ben has "flown" halfway round the world. More importantly, he has relaxed physically and mentally. Sometimes he even falls asleep for a few minutes and wakes refreshed and ready to go on.

There are a number of ways to teach your children how to relax, ranging from mental imagery to exercise, stretching, deep-muscle relaxation, and so on. Some excellent books on this subject are listed in the Suggested Reading section at the back of this book. You may also want to ask your child's school librarian or the local public librarian for additional resource suggestions.

Teaching Your Children How to Manage Stress

The ability to manage stress is especially necessary in a youngster's life since so much of a child's existence involves continual change, clarification of values, and forced choices. Unexpected or unfamiliar situations requiring as-yet-unlearned coping skills produce a great deal of stress for children. Children who learn how to deal effectively with the stress and strains of everyday life are likely to be healthy and happy and have a zest and zeal for living. By learning the goals and principles of coping, children can draw vitality from stress and use it constructively.

How children will deal with stress as adults is determined to a great extent by what happens during their most impressionable formative years. Studies have shown how important these early experiences are in influencing later behavior. The more we know about the stresses and strains of childhood, and the more we help our children develop the skills to deal with them, the better able they are to use these skills now and in later years. Be alert for the symptoms that show your child is experiencing stress. When a youngster exhibits physical, emotional, or behavioral symptoms that are inappropriate or unhealthy (such as fighting, swearing, hostility, or psychosomatic illness— persistent stomachaches or headaches), it's time to find out the cause. Watch closely for stress signs that show the child is not coping well, and then get help if you feel you need assistance. School counselors, your family doctor, and your child's pediatrician are all potential sources of help.

Learn about the "normal" stresses, strains, and fears of childhood. Many are predictable at the various ages and stages of childhood. Take the time to know what they are for your child's age group. When you reduce your children's insecurities, they are less emotionally encumbered. There are a number of books that can teach you how to help your children learn how to manage stress. Some are listed in the Suggested Reading section. You might also want to ask your child's school counselor or librarian for additional resources.

The unknown produces fears. This is true for children of all ages. These anxieties keep children from the work to be done in childhood, like making and sustaining friends, learning, and self-discovery. Take the time to read and discuss with other parents and professionals about childhood. This helps you understand a great deal about your child's needs. For example, we know that the development of the five-year-old doesn't include the capacity to separate reality from fantasy. If a young child imagines a ghost is in the room, you don't hide the ghost under the bed, or behind the headboard. You suggest the ghost is up in the corner (so to speak) where your child can "see" it. Then you give it a friendly name and tell your child that it's there for protection. We create a fantasy to help deal with it because the child doesn't have the capacity to make the fear go away. That's why the world of fantasy and imagination is used so often in early childhood. It helps children make fears manageable.

Monitoring your children's television viewing can do a lot to avoid some of the stress children experience. Having erased the dividing line between childhood and adulthood programming, television exposes children to hostile images that disrupt their physical and emotional safety—images beyond what many are capable of handling. That's why you *must* censure your child's television viewing in the early years. I advise parents to monitor television viewing until their children are at least twelve years old. Up to this time, children are fairly agreeable about watching prerecorded (or rented or purchased) videos, so you have a good deal of control in monitoring what they are watching. For older children, point out how violent news can be necessarily disturbing, how a scary movie may cause them to be frightened, how positive images create good feelings and can bring about feelings of happiness, and so on. Explain the importance of protecting their minds from unnecessary hostile and violent images (this goes for music lyrics). Harmful insecurities are created as a result of the impact of these images on young minds.

Safeguarding our children's health is one of the most important tasks of parenting. By exhibiting good habits, including eating properly, exercising regularly, and taking time out for relaxation and managing stress, we teach our children to take responsibility for their health and wellness.

5

Will Your Children Say No to Alcohol and Drugs?

O ne of the most daunting tasks parents face is getting their children through childhood without their succumbing to alcohol and drugs. Substance and chemical abuse can alter our children's lives forever. Keeping our children drug and alcohol free is no easy task. Growing up in contemporary society calls for an ever-increasing ability to endure anxiety, tolerate tension, overcome doubt, resolve conflicts, reduce frustrations, manage stress, and avoid peer and external pressures.

Coping Through Chemicals

Today's young people are more likely to use drugs and alcohol than any age group before them and to do so at a far younger age. Even if they have never smoked marijuana, taken pills that were not prescribed for them, or used cocaine themselves, most young people know someone who has. Drug use is all around them, from the adult who takes tranquilizers to cope with daily stress, to youngsters who sell pot at school, to movie idols who glamorize drug use on-screen and off. The result has been an increased acceptability of drug use over the last decade, making it a rite of passage, the difference between being part of the crowd and an outsider. Like an adult who has a drink "just to be sociable," a child will share a drug with a friend; others use drugs to escape from what they consider intolerable lives; still others use them "because they're there." It's estimated that over one third of all U.S. adolescents use alcohol and illegal drugs.

The progression of drug use often moves through what is generally referred to as "gateway drugs": first the legal ones, alcohol and tobacco, then on to marijuana and other more harmful and addictive drugs. Polydrug addiction is common; its common denominator is alcohol. If children begin to drink, the possibility increases that they will also use one or more drugs. Once drug or alcohol involvement begins, it can accelerate quickly, moving from occasional indulgence to dependence. Children, even more so than adults, are susceptible to this snowball effect. Ramon, a high school student tells it this way.

> Drug dependence is a strange thing. You're sure that you have everything under control, that you only use drugs occasionally, you know, when you need them to help you handle the bad times in school and when your friends abandon you. But gradually you get pulled in. At the beginning of ninth grade, I started to get high every morning when I arrived at school, and some days I'd just never make it to classes. Soon I decided my old friends were boring so I turned to older kids who were more exciting. Besides, the older guys had cars. Since I always had money and shared it

for beer and grass they were all too happy to have me along. They introduced me to wild parties and good times. But it was a bad move. The friends I hung around with weren't real friends—they were just convenient. I used them and they used me. I wouldn't hesitate to steal drugs or money from them, and they'd do the same with me. So there was no one I could trust. I started losing self-respect. I no longer cared how I dressed or whether my hair was too long, or how I talked in front of people. I made the soccer team each year, but often went to practice stoned and just sat on the sidelines.

It was a vicious cycle. I would do drugs to feel better about myself, but I'd end up feeling worse, so I'd do more drugs. Getting high was no longer a thing I did to feel happy and have fun. It was a part of my life. I had to get high just to feel normal and not drained and burned out. The drugs had flattened everything out.

My last cry for help was when I got in trouble with the law and my parents were called to pick me up from the police station for disturbing the peace. I know it sounds crazy, but I was so relieved. I had been rescued. I would no longer need my big-guy/tough-guy act.

Your *Child Is at Risk, Too*

As parents you can't afford to be naive about substance and chemical abuse. You may be caring, emotionally and physically accessible, not drink or use drugs, yet your children may encounter and use drugs just the same. Every young person needs to learn the possible effects of alcohol and drug use on one's health and learn ways to withstand the extraordinary pressures for using them. Those who do not are at risk. Anything that accentuates the self-doubt that kids harbor about themselves or their abilities may subtly or inadvertently lead to alcohol or drug use. Factors that make a child vulnerable to the influence of alcohol and drugs include:

- Divorce, separation, or remarriage of parents
- Death of a parent, sibling, or friend
- Home or school relocation
- Loss of a long-standing friendship or love relationship
- Major tests or exams
- Poor self-image
- Family discord
- Sexual or physical abuse
- Lack of emotional and physical affection by parents
- Disharmony in the child-parent relationship
- Parents who smoke, drink, use illegal drugs, or abuse prescription drugs

Is Your Child Using? How You Can Tell

Parents often see many clues that they ignore, hoping they will go away. Don't. No one knows the intricate habits and patterns of your child quite like you do. No one can detect changes as you can. Watch for these abrupt changes.

Peer group. The child suddenly starts hanging out with a new group, spending a lot of time with new friends you do not meet and never hear much about.

Personality. Your child may suddenly have extreme bouts of hostility, avoidance of family contact, moodiness, wild elation, depression, or a "get off my back; leave me alone" attitude toward you or other family members.

School performance. Tardiness, a sudden decline in grades, or the onset of absenteeism should not be overlooked or dismissed.

Handling responsibilities. Watch for noticeable and persistent neglect of chores or routine responsibilities, or work done carelessly.

Physical appearance. There may be a sudden change in physical characteristics, such as reddened or bloodshot eyes, dark glasses worn indoors, persistent use of eye drops, persistent cough, vomiting, frequent listlessness, drowsy behavior, staggering, morning headaches, weight loss or loss of appetite, peculiar odor on breath and clothes. Be aware of unusual smells, such as burning incense to mask odors.

Disappearing items. Watch for signs indicating disappearance of prescription pills from the medicine chest; tablets and capsules among the child's possessions; repeated requests to borrow money; unexplained disappearance of cash, cameras, radios, jewelry, or other valuable possessions convertible to money for drugs; large supplies of rubber cement and glue or glue-stained plastic bags; bottles of cough medicine containing narcotics; bent spoons, syringes, eyedroppers, and cotton balls; a persistent sweet or lingering odor on clothing.

Is Your Child Drinking? How You Can Tell

These clues apply specifically to alcohol use.

Family liquor. Is the liquor supply dwindling? If your child is abusing alcohol, your stock might evaporate mysteriously or turn into colored water. Unless you keep an inventory of your liquor, such practices may go undetected for months.

Neighborhood reports. Do I hear consistently from neighbors, friends, or others about my child's drinking or questionable behavior? An alcoholic youngster's reputation suffers. Listen to these warnings.

Police. Is my child in trouble with the police? Even one arrest for an alcohol-related offense is a red flag that may well signal alcoholism.

Attitude change. Does my youngster turn off to talks about alcohol or strongly defend the right to use it?

Is Your Child Smoking? How You Can Tell

Most young people are well aware of the danger of smoking cigarettes. They also know that parents do not want them to smoke. Apparently these deterrents fail, because it is reported that 67 percent of all junior and senior high school youngsters smoke two or three cigarettes every day. Research shows that virtually all sixth- and seventh-grade kids try smoking at least once, but half lose interest without going beyond the experimental stage. It's estimated that of the 50 percent left, more than half will become serious smokers (smoking one or more packs a day) by the time they are in ninth grade. Experts warn that the most vulnerable period for addiction is in mid-adolescence.

These specific clues suggest your children are smoking.

Cover-ups. Are my children buying and using a lot of room deodorizer (to get rid of the scent of cigarettes), breath mints, and breath spray (to get the scent off their breath)?

Pilfering. Am I missing a few cigarettes here and there out of my own packs, or missing a pack every now and then from a carton?

Peer smoking. Do most of my children's friends smoke? Although that's not a definite sign that your children smoke, peer pressure is a very strong thing. If a boyfriend or girlfriend smokes, it is even more likely that your child will smoke.

Arguments. Have my children become belligerent when I talk to them about smoking, calling me a hypocrite for continuing to lecture them about how bad smoking is while I go through a pack or two a day?

Hero worship. Do my children have heroes, rock stars or actors, who smoke?

Can You Help Your Children to "Just Say No"?

The discovery that your child is using drugs or alcohol is a soul-shaking experience. After the initial response of shock and outrage, you may be tempted to react with pity and indulgence or with rejection and even physical punishment. Don't. These responses will not be helpful either to you or your child. Parents are still the first and best line of defense. "Parents have to take primary responsibility for their family's education about drugs and what drugs do their kids," says Joyce Nalepka, former president of the National Federation of Parents for Drug-Free Youth. It's not enough merely to tell kids to say no. You have to explain the dangers and give your kids mental ammunition and skills to combat the pressures to use drugs. Here are steps you can take to help your child *want* to avoid substance and chemical use.

Be a positive role model. Treat a nondrinking guest with respect, and don't pressure anyone to "have another." Don't create the impression that the only way to socialize is with a drink. Don't intimate that alcohol or pills are to be used to relax, alleviate anxiety, or counteract depression, melancholy, or tiredness.

Don't glamorize drinking or taking drugs. Don't praise someone else's tolerance by telling stories about the guest who "drank everyone under the table," or used drugs as a way to relax. Explain that while alcohol is enjoyed socially to accentuate a good meal or celebrate a special event, it is not a prerequisite.

Communicate. Provide the honest facts about alcohol and drugs. Scare tactics or hysterical exaggerations should not be used. Share your values and point out what is and isn't legal.

Get to know your child's friends and their parents. Provide responsible supervision at your house when your child has friends over; when your child is spending the evening at a friend's house, check with the parents to see that an adult will be supervising.

Be aware of the early signs of drug and alcohol abuse. You need to get help for the family as well as the child. Speak with your community pharmacist, who is an expert on drugs and their effects on humans. A number of resources are listed at the back of this book, and you can check with your public library for additional resources.

Encourage activities that can give a natural high. Sports, recreation, spiritual support, and volunteer activities can help channel the need for risk and fun and be real substitutes for drugs.

Participate. Form groups with other concerned parents. Join your PTA. Invite drug counselors to meetings. Talk with school superintendents, principals, coaches, physicians, church personnel, and local politicians to make sure that everyone is not only aware of drug problems but are responsive to them and concerned about prevention as well as intervention tactics in your community.

Commend businesses that enforce No Smoking rules. We need all the help we can get in sending the message of being responsible about alcohol and chemical use. Applaud those who do.

What to Do When You Know Your Child Is Using Drugs

This is one time when the ostrich attitude can be lethal. If you look the other way, you can only expect the problem to get worse. Confront your child. A forthright dialogue is absolutely essential. Help your child see the necessity of licking the habit early on, because it's so pernicious. Here are the ground rules:

1. Do not discuss the matter when the child is high on drugs or alcohol. Whatever you say will not get through.
2. When your child is back to normal and you can talk calmly, show your concern and ask questions. What is happening? Why?
3. Listen without interrupting.
4. Examine your own attitude about drugs and alcohol. Is it possible you are sending conflicting messages?
5. Confront the problem. When you see signs of trouble, don't look the other way or, worse yet, show pity. At this stage, your child needs your help, not your tolerance and acceptance. Real parental love may best be demonstrated by guiding a child toward self-help. Teach your child to develop the strength to find other constructive ways of dealing with these problems and feelings. If you find your child's problem is too much for you to handle, seek help. Information about Alcoholics Anonymous as well as other excellent programs is given at the back of this book.

The best ammunition parents have to safeguard our children against the ravages of alcohol and drugs is the attitudes and skills we help our children acquire.

6

Do Your Children Feel Safe at School?

The length of time adults will stay in a job is often determined by whether or not the environment is safe and orderly. This perception of safety also affects the level of performance and productivity, the trust an employee has in fellow workers, and how much respect and support is given to supervisors. Individuals who do not feel safe while at work are more prone to depression and mood swings, have the highest absenteeism rate, file a great many more insurance claims than do their coworkers, and are more likely to try to cope by using drugs or alcohol.

Children, Like Adults, Go to Work Each Day

School is your child's workplace. Your work environment and your child's workplace are surprisingly similar. Children must confront people, projects, and pressures. Learning is tough stuff, and the atmosphere is often one of competition and challenge. Your child will spend a great deal of time in the school environment over the course of a thirteen-year education. You should know about your children's safety there. School isn't always the fun and easy experience we might like to believe it is.

Why School Safety Is Your Concern

Many children are fearful while they are in school or at school-related functions. Children are most distressed when they fear another student, when school activities are not well supervised, and when they hear about an incident of violence or are themselves the victims of violence. It's not uncommon for young children to fear the unknown disciplinary techniques a teacher may use "if I'm not good." Even older children who are timid or shy can be fearful of a teacher and of classmates. These fears have repercussions. Countless parents have told me about children who, after being enrolled in school, begin stuttering, bed-wetting, nail biting, thumb sucking, having nightmares, or complaining of headaches and stomachaches. These stress responses are physical reactions to being emotionally fearful.

Why Children Fear Going to School

Two large eighth-grade boys came up to Trinh one day, pushed him into a locker, shoved him around, and demanded his lunch money. They threatened to beat him up unless he gave them all his money that day and a dollar every day from then on. They told him where to meet them and said to wrap the money in a piece of notebook paper. Trinh handed over his money the first time and tried to ignore them the next day. They singled him out, slammed him around, and threatened him. He began giving them money every day. He was afraid to tell anyone. He didn't know that the same boys were doing the same thing to several other students in his class. Everyone was too afraid to talk, and the bullies prospered.

Girls are not immune from fears for their physical safety either. Ten-year-old Lael became angry at her best friend Gwen one day and shoved her, making her fall down. As Lael was about to apologize, Gwen picked herself up off the floor and, with a frightened look on her face, apologized for irritating Lael. Lael was surprised, but she enjoyed the feeling of power. Soon, seeing that she could often get whatever she wanted by bullying, Lael began using physical abuse on other children. The other little girls were afraid of Lael, who would pull their hair or step on their feet, but were afraid to say anything. Lael got away with more and more as the other children became increasingly frightened of annoying or bothering her.

These things can happen to very small children too. Fourth-grader Sam innocently walked into the school rest room one afternoon, interrupting some sixth-grade boys who were smoking. Shoving him up against the wall, they threatened to burn him with the cigarette. When he began crying, they made fun of him and shoved him on the floor. Although Sam promised not to tell anyone of the incident, the older boys made a point of glaring at him whenever they came across him at recess or in the cafeteria. Sam was terrified and had trouble concentrating for weeks.

It's no wonder that children are frightened. According to National Institute of Education statistics on school safety for 1986, American secondary schools reported 282,000 physical attacks, 112,000 robberies in which force or threats were used, 2,400,000 thefts of personal property, and 2,400 fires in a typical month. Over 800,000 students missed school because they were too afraid to attend. Even teachers were not immune to violence: 1,000 teachers—and remember this is in one month—were assaulted seriously enough to require medical attention. And violence escalates every year. While we like to think we are sending our children off to a safe and secure environment, this is not always true. Children have good reason to feel increasingly unsafe.

Are Your Children Eager to Go to School?

It isn't always something violent that creates an atmosphere of fear at school. Jean was a happy third-grader, enjoying school, chattering every day about what was going to happen the next day. One week, she stopped talking about school. Soon she began complaining of being tired and saying that she didn't like school. Concerned, her parents talked to Jean's teacher. They found out that Jean was being teased by two little girls in her class who pinched her all the time. Jean had started it, teasing the girls who wore green on Thursday ("That means you're a nerd!") Jean pinched the girls once, and they never let her forget it. They pinched her back, hard, every chance they got. Jean complained to the teacher, who told the other girls to stop the pinching. Instead, they pinched harder and got some of the other kids to join in. Even those kids in the class who liked Jean began pinching her, because it was the thing to do. Jean began to fear going to class.

In addition to the obvious seriousness of being a victim of a crime, all students are indirectly but seriously affected by the threat of physical or emotional harm in school.

The child who views the school as a hostile environment is likely to dislike school, the teachers, and fellow students. Students who are afraid at school are more likely to rate themselves as below-average students and actually do receive lower grades. Fear reduces their ability to concentrate on schoolwork and creates an atmosphere of mistrust. It undermines morale and teaches that the staff is not in control; student disorder is more powerful than the adult call for order. Students who are attacked without provocation or who do not know their assailants—and the majority of assaults are of this type—experience the greatest prolonged levels of anxiety, stress, and depression.

Children who have been victims of attack, robbery, or verbal abuse often admit that they are afraid on the way to and from school and while they are actually in school. If their uneasiness becomes intolerable, they will stay away from school altogether. In 1990, more than one million children dropped out of school, according to the National Dropout Center, and the figure continues to increase. To what extent is personal safety a factor?

Many students are unable to strike back when they become the target of violence or hostility. These children are most susceptible to stress-related illness because they have an impaired ability to deal effectively with fear or anger. Instead, they internalize their fear or rage. Remember, children don't receive training to prepare them for the threat of violence and abuse in school, and many are ill-equipped to confront the dangers they find there.

Making Sure Your Children Feel Safe at School

School safety is *your* concern. Making sure your children go to school is not enough. Here's what you can do.

Be aware. Be aware of your children's fears and anxieties about physical safety. Don't underestimate or ignore the fears a child may be experiencing; the expectation of a stressful event can be every bit as potent as the event it-self. Adolescents, like young children, need to feel they can turn to trusted adults for help when it's needed. This reduces the feelings of helplessness. Teach your children what to do, what to say, and where to turn for help should they encounter situations that cause fears while at school. The areas in school buildings that account for some of the big fears include:

- The rest rooms: Children fear encountering other students there who will rough them up in order to make them keep secrets (from the school staff or other students) about their using drugs or smoking.
- The bus: Children fear rowdy, aggressive, and verbal-ly abusive students who force them to leave a favored seat or rough them up just for the fun of it.
- The empty hallway: Children fear encountering the school tough guys while they are walking alone.
- The lunchroom: Children fear being shoved, poked, or pushed out of their place in line or having food thrown at them by another student.
- The unsupervised classroom or hallway: Children fear getting into a fight with another student and be-ing hurt or embarrassed in front of their peers.
- The principal's office: All children, even the tough guys, fear going to the office when discipline is the issue.

There are also certain types of people that students fear. These include:

- Bullies: Every school has its tough guys and tough girls, who seem to enjoy picking on those who show fear.

- Foreign students: Some students are afraid to be around people they can't understand, those who speak another language, fearing that these students are talking about and making fun of them.
- Teachers: Some teachers project a very stern image, making them scary just to look at or think about, even though they may be gentle people once you get to know them.

Don't hesitate to intervene. Children who want the attention and admiration of older children may become willing victims, often giving up money or objects in exchange for group friendship. Don't let your child struggle in an unhealthy environment without intervening. Many fathers tell me they think their children (especially sons) should be left alone to solve their own problems because it "builds character." That's simply not the case. It's more likely to lead to feelings of abandonment, fear, depression, and mistrust.

Take your child seriously. Though an incident may not seem serious to you, it's the child's perception that counts. Listen to the story, and then decide how to help. Many young people face undue harassment by another student and either cannot resolve it or are afraid to. If this is happening to your child, it may mean a lack of certain self-management skills such as assertiveness. Assertiveness training, problem solving, and conflict management skills are all worth learning (assertiveness and problem solving are discussed in later chapters). They can add to your child's feelings of self-protection. You may want to check your local community education programs for workshops and courses in these areas. There are also a number of books on these topics for parents and children. The Suggested Reading section at the back of this book highlights a few, and you may want to ask the librarian at your local public library or your child's school to suggest others. Don't hesitate to talk with the school's counselors, nurse, or principal, or with other parents, about your concerns.

Learn about classroom rules, policies, and procedures. The rules designed to govern physical safety in the classroom send a message loud and clear that all children are protected there. No doubt your child's teacher has certain rules posted for all students to observe. Rules like "No running, shoving, hitting" as well as other safety rules (what to do in case of a fire or other emergencies) make it clear to each student that the teacher values the safety of all the children in the room. Be sure that your child knows what the rules are (and why and how they are designed to protect) and follows them.

Learn about the policies that govern school-wide safety. What rules exist for student safety in the school environment? Again, be sure your child knows the rules, and follows them. If rules are lacking or not enforced, arrange a time to meet with the principal and your PTA to discuss what can be done.

Learn about school security. Security procedures are necessary in every school. The best ones are unobtrusive, of course. Measures to ensure physical security must focus on guaranteeing internal control of the school and external control of its perimeter. Take the time to talk to the school principal, grounds keeper, or security officer about what safety measures are being used on your child's school campus. Are there guards, or do teachers regularly walk through corridors and grounds? Does a patrol car come by to check the parking lot during evening activities? Is the campus well lit at night?

School personnel will usually be willing to tell you about security measures. If they are not, you might take their reluctance as a tacit admission that the school's security measures are not as good as they should be. If you can't get any information from the school, call the local police department to find out whether there have been any crime reports filed from the school and, if so, how many and of what type.

If security is inadequate, help change it. If you are displeased, say so. Tell the principal, superintendent, or members of the school board. If you can't get any satisfaction, consider an editorial in the newspaper or ask a local television station to investigate. Ask your community to back programs to make your schools a safer place. The effort may have to begin with you.

Ask your children about their teachers. Listen to the stories your children share. Concentrate on their tone of voice. Do your children sound truly frightened, upset, insecure? Do they seem embarrassed when talking about something the teacher said or did? Do they sound as if they are covering up anything? Ask about how other children in the class view the teacher. Sexual abuse or mental cruelty have a devastating effect even on children who are not directly involved.

Take the time to find out how your children are doing at school and to discuss what brings them distress. There is usually a reason behind every insecurity. Talking about it with your children shows them you care and are taking steps to protect them. You make them feel more secure. Until your children feel physically secure, they are not free to develop the normal curiosity and excitement about the rest of their life.

III

Helping Your Children Feel Secure Emotionally

7

Happiness: How Children and Parents Differ on Its Meaning

Swedish psychoanalyst Stefi Pedersen guided a group of refugees who were escaping from the Nazis in Norway into Sweden. The escape was made over mountains in the wintertime by a group that included several small children. Because the climb was difficult, the elements harsh, and speed essential, the rule was that people could take only what they could carry. Many in the group had fled the Nazis previously and knew to take only the barest of possessions.

After crossing the Swedish border, the group finally was able to take a break and have a meal. At that point, Pedersen happened to look into the knapsack of one of the children and found, to her surprise, a small silver star, such as people hang on Christmas trees. As a child psychologist, Pedersen was interested in what might provide psychological safety to a child and checked the packs of the other children to see what possessions they valued most. Bag after bag contained inexpensive Christmas tree decorations, some made just from cardboard and glitter. Most of the children were Jewish but had celebrated Christmas as a secular children's holiday. Pedersen concluded that the Christmas decorations were symbolic of their happy past and were taken to provide a feeling of safety as they set off on a trip into the unknown. The symbols of the happiness they had once known with their families in their own homes eased their feelings of loneliness and helplessness, offering them the promise of hope. When you think about your children's emotional security and well-being, what comes to mind?

When I ask parents what they want most for their children, most respond with "Happiness. We want our children to be happy." We all want our children to be healthy, happy, well-adjusted, and secure in our love. As parents, we do everything in our power to see to it that they are. We provide shelter and security; we care for their immediate needs and seek to give things they want—sometimes doing without in order that our children can have more. We tickle, say nonsensical and silly things, make funny faces to make our children giggle, don a clown suit to entertain at a birthday party or a Santa Claus suit at Christmastime. We want to see our children be happy.

Happiness is not just an outward expression. It's an internal state of affairs. Happiness is not like a deferred payment plan—"I'll be happy when I have a new toy, bike, car; can do what I want, have my own way." Happiness is practiced in the present. As the saying goes, "You carry your sunshine with you."

How can we gauge our children's true sense of inner happiness and not just see what our loving and hopeful eyes want to see? How can we help our children develop an inner harmony so genuine it radiates outward? Once again, parents are the key. Keeping our children emotionally happy has a lot to do with understanding the nature of children, to make sure they feel our love and help them learn to nurture their own well-being.

The Work of Childhood

Just as children can annoy parents to the point of being angry, we can do that to our children as well. Have you ever baited your children into needless frustration and negative behavior that could have been avoided? We all do this from time to time, but when we understand the dynamics behind a child's actions, when we understand the psychology of children, we can better minimize the chances of this happening.

How do we know when to turn the other cheek and "not hear" the under-the-breath comment and when to jump into the middle of an issue and wrestle it out until we come to an agreement? Understanding the stages of child development and knowing how each manifests itself in our children's behavior can be a big help. The work of each stage is pretty well defined. Each presents its own set of tasks and demands, all focused on gaining self-knowledge—selfhood. We know, for example, that at age fourteen a child's primary need is for unconditional acceptance as an individual. Fourteen-year-olds want to be accepted, no matter what. Long hair, purple hair, or no hair, their actions will center on gaining approval and total acceptance for their individual sense of self. The goal is to win their parents' acceptance on these terms. They try a similar tactic with friends and peers, without alienating them because they need their acceptance too. We call this necessary and natural developmental stage "seeking autonomy." Fourteen-year-olds differ from five-year-olds whose primary need is to be with their parents, preferably all the time. They'd like to spend the daytime hours with them and sleep in their room at night. Their greatest fear is to be *without* them. They'll need a heavy dose of parental security because the next stage is to trust themselves as separate and capable of accomplishment in their own right. We call this necessary and natural developmental stage "separation anxiety." Whereas fourteen-year-olds seek separation from their parents, five-year-olds are debilitated by it.

By understanding the work or task of each year of life in the childhood years, you can better understand a child's needs and subsequent behavior and help your children learn appropriate ways to respond to people and events. Such insight helps you to decipher how the work involved at each stage of growing up influences your child's perception of self. For example, up to the age of two, children primarily view themselves as part of their mother (or father if he is the primary caretaker). Upon reaching two, they develop the ability to be aware that they are, in reality, separate. This presents the task of establishing autonomy—separateness. The two words that best describe this newfound selfhood are *no* and *mine*. Possession is a tool used to enforce that sense of separate self. In other words, two-year-olds are looking for power and ways to assert it. Effective parenting is a matter of giving them choices. Let them pick out which shoes to wear or how to comb their hair. Let them decide which book you are going to read aloud. In each instance, provide two or three choices, all of which you can live with.

Age three is about mastery. Having realized their separateness, three-year-olds go on to master their environment. Mastery plays an important role in the perception of self; it influences the feeling of being capable (or not capable). The need for success in their endeavors at this stage is crucial. Three-year-olds labor over each accomplishment. They are slow and methodical, and it takes forever to do each task. Needing feedback to know if they have been successful, they strive for recognition of these achievements ("Watch me, Mommy! Watch me, Daddy!"). Here, effective parenting is about recognizing these achievements and encouraging performance. Praise with tangible signs such as putting drawings on the refrigerator or around the house. Stimulate their intellect and curiosity by questioning. Ask your daughter to tell you how or why she has drawn a certain picture, or why she has chosen to use certain colors in the picture. Be patient as you answer her repeated questions. The search for mastery stimulates curiosity. "Why, why, why?" she wants to know. Her drive for discovering is insatiable; her capacity for learning is unlimited.

It's also a time of gaining a sense of their own maleness or femaleness. Here the opposite-sex parent plays a major role in the child's sense of self: Boys prefer time with their mother, girls with their father.

Ages seven to eight are about sameness. Children want to feel a oneness with their same-age, same-sex peers. Playmates are the new "reflectors." Friends are all-important. Children of this age should be encouraged to join same-age groups, provided with opportunities to develop skills in a variety of activities, and helped to learn healthy and positive ways to relate to others—namely, acquiring and maintaining friendships. Teach and reinforce the skills of fairness and cooperation. This is a great age to begin activities such as Girl Scouts or Boy Scouts or other similar activities that encourage same-age same-sex friendships.

Ages thirteen to fifteen are about verifying a sense of self-worth and coping with growing pains. Physical maturation—internal and external—occurs at an amazing rate. Key hormones are at work now, doing their job of moving children from preadolescence to full-scale puberty. The offshoot of such erratic physical growth is an awkwardness coupled with emotional upheavals. These children often feel alone. You can best help them by discussing these changes, reassuring them that they are normal and natural. Talk about your child's emotional ups and downs and how to deal with them. Keep your focus on building a positive and mutual relationship between the two of you. What you do now will set the tone for your relationship over the next few years. This is a good time to learn effective ways to listen so your child will talk, and talk so your child will listen. This is important because the next stage of development has to do with establishing a workable and meaningful philosophy of life. Reevaluating moral concepts will mean searching for the child's own personal beliefs, complete with facing religious, ethical, and value-laden ideologies. Developing personal convictions and committing to them is all-important—especially if there is conflict between what the child believes, what the child was raised with, and what the peer group finds acceptable.

Learn about your children's stages of development, and talk with them, giving them a sense of understanding themselves and their motivations. This is especially important in the adolescent years, when development is so mysterious to teens, yet it is a period when they sincerely want to know what is going on. There are a number of good books for parents and their children that can help you learn more about your children, and how to help your children learn more about themselves. The Suggested Reading section at the back of this book provides resources, and you may wish to consult your local public library for additional information. The more we know about our children, the better we are able to prepare them for adulthood.

Children Develop in a Sequential Way

From the overview of the several stages provided here, you can see two obvious outcomes. First, childhood is about change, and second, childhood unfolds in sequential fashion. Whether your child is five or fourteen, seven or sixteen, take time to learn about the characteristics of that stage. This gives you insight into a child's aspirations and motivations and provides you with information you can use in maintaining a harmonious relationship throughout it, and helping develop the skills to overcome the stress and strains encountered along the way.

Children are always in transition—always moving from one developmental stage to the next. To that end, you might think of a child as a person who:

- Is leaving behind an earlier stage of development and is moving along to the next developmental stage.
- When scared or frightened, slips back into the security of the previous stage; when feeling secure, ventures on to try on the trappings of the next stage.
- Is undergoing a rapid and intense period of physiological and psychological changes.
- Wants to be independent but doesn't have a backlog of personal experiences to use in functioning independently.

- Needs to express needs and to have these needs taken seriously.
- Has not yet formed a cohesive value system that would suggest what to "live for," so this tremendously important anchor of security is not yet within reach.
- Is locked into financial and emotional dependence on the family.
- Notices when there are discrepancies between the rules and values claimed by adults and adult behavior.
- Has the same intense emotional needs and feelings as adults, with limited understanding as to what these emotions mean or how to cope successfully with them (until taught to do so).
- Has a strong need for adult guidance in constructing a separate identity and tries to acquire a sustaining sense of selfhood.
- Feels lonely and alone when parents are physically and emotionally absent; needs them to show love and attention, listen and show empathy and patience, offer guidance and direction, allow experiences for positive growth through exploration, encourage separation and independence, help cope with the crisis at hand, model what it's like to be an adult.
- Without adult nurturing, becomes unable to construct a secure self-identity and becomes less competent to meet the challenges inevitable in daily life.
- In the absence of adaptive coping skills, becomes debilitated by the ravages of stress.
- When the family situation does not feel nurturing or supportive, feels helpless and turns to peers for the fulfillment of these needs.

Television and Emotional Health

Next to the family, television is probably the most important influence on children in our society. Research by the American Academy of Pediatrics (AAP) shows that by high school graduation the average adolescent will have spent more time in front of a television set than in the classroom. The AAP believes that excessive television viewing can be linked with violent and aggressive behavior, obesity, poor academic performance, precocious sexuality, and the use of drugs and alcohol on the part of our children. It's important that parents help children to use television as a positive, creative force and avoid television's negative influences. Consider the following.

Time. Children in the United States spend three to five hours a day watching television, which means that the time available for other activities is severely limited. Childhood is a period of growth and development. Children need to play, alone and with other children; play is a way of learning valuable physical, mental, and social skills. Children need to read, talk, and interact with other children and adults. Television viewing frequently occupies time that could be devoted to these other pursuits. Yet television rarely promotes the physical, mental, and social skills that enhance the transition to adulthood.

Exposure to violence. The amount of violence shown on television is increasing. Viewing violent programs may encourage your children's tendency toward aggression. Parents who watch television with their children will be able to point out that violence on television is not real and that the actor has not actually been killed or maimed. Parents can also disapprove of the violent episodes and stress that such behavior is not the best way to resolve a problem. By discussing the violence shown on television, parents can lessen its impact. The best solution, of course, is for parents to eliminate the most violent programs from their children's schedule.

School performance. Many recent studies suggest that excessive television viewing may have a detrimental effect on learning and school performance. The hours spent viewing television interfere with homework and limit the time available for other ways of learning. If a child is not performing well academically, the many mindless hours in front of the television set may be a strong factor contributing to the problem.

Sexuality, drugs, and alcohol. Television exposes children to adult behaviors in ways that suggest that these are normal and risk-free. Sexual behavior and the use of alcohol or drugs are often portrayed in inviting terms. Because of the frequency with which these behaviors occur on television, the message seems to be that "everyone does it." Television characters rarely say no. Ten percent of adolescent girls in the United States get pregnant each year. The leading cause of death in teenage boys is accidents, 50 percent of which involve alcohol. Although television viewing is not the only way that children learn about sexuality and drug and alcohol use, the risks of these behaviors are not given equal time. The types of behavior on cable television are even more extreme.

Suggestions through commercials. According to the American Academy of Pediatrics, the average child sees more than twenty thousand commercials during the thirteen hundred to fourteen hundred hours of television that he or she views annually. AAP research on television and the family shows that advertisers spend roughly $700 million a year to make sure that their sales pitches reach large numbers of children. More than 60 percent of the commercials are for cereal, candy, or toys. Among the top TV advertisers are a number of corporations that aim all or most of their sales efforts at children.

The majority of food advertising is for heavily sugared products such as candy and presweetened cereals. Commercials for meat, milk products, bread, and juice make up only about 4 percent of the food ads shown during children's viewing time. This emphasis gives children a distorted picture of how they ought to eat. Ads that are often more entertaining than the programs themselves suggest that the way to eat is by snacking and eating sugary foods.

In prime-time TV, eating is a frequent occurrence. According to the AAP, the amount of television watched is directly related to the child's number and kind of snacks. It is therefore not surprising that a direct relationship has been found between increased television viewing and children's risk of being overweight.

What You Can Do to Control TV Viewing

Set limits. First, know how many hours of television your children watch. Limit and guide your children's viewing. Lock-out devices are available so that certain channels, such as pornographic channels on cable television, cannot be seen. Remember that before television, families had no trouble finding other means of growth and entertainment.

Your children probably won't like being kept away from the television set. However, establishing good habits for your children is worth the effort. Television watching is often more habit than choice. It is said that TV watching is addictive. Don't be surprised if your children go through a sort of withdrawal when their television time is reduced. You can ease the transition by encouraging activities such as sports, games, chores, reading, conversation, or hobbies. You can help even more by joining your children in these activities. One television newsman, for example, had his children write short reports on all programs they watched. Not only did this reduce their viewing, it also helped to develop their critical thinking and writing skills. Because children model their behavior after their parents' example, an examination of your own television viewing habits may also help.

Plan. When you limit TV time, your children will need to plan their viewing to get the most enjoyment out of their time. Use of a TV guide or newspaper listing is preferable to flipping channels to decide what to watch. The set should go on only for specific programs, and it should go off when they are over. Approach a television program as you would a movie. Decide which show to see and talk about it after it ends. Do not use television viewing to reward or withhold it to punish your children. Such practices make television seem even more important.

Participate. Childhood is the time when children begin to learn the strategies they need to live in the world. You are their most important example. Television is their second most important source of information. Children will learn the most from how you interpret the TV programs you see together. Watch television with them and talk about what you see. This may help you to discuss topics that may be difficult: family life, love, sex, war, work. The worst program might be a good experience for your children if you are there to help them get the right message, while the best program might be wasted without your encouragement to think, evaluate, and question what was seen. If you are offended by certain programs and intend to forbid your children to watch them, try to communicate your reasons. Remember, it is your job to interpret what your children see on TV. If your children are already watching a program and see behavior to which you object, tell them so and explain why.

Resist commercials. Don't expect your children to resist commercials for candy and snack food without help from you. The ability to see though a sales pitch is learned fairly late and with difficulty, but poor eating habits can be picked up early and with ease. Good habits formed in childhood are the foundation of good health habits in adulthood. The advertisers have market researchers, writers, producers, and saturation campaigns with big budgets on their side; they fight hard to deliver their messages. When your children request foods and toys advertised on television, teach them how television makes them want things they don't necessarily need, which may even be harmful.

Express your views. An effective way to change commercials or programs is to call your local television station. When you are offended or pleased by something on television, let the station manager know. Write or call the network or the program's sponsor. Stations, networks, and sponsors are all concerned about the effects of television on children and are responsible to parents' concerns. Be specific. Don't call or write just to complain. It is also important to voice your approval. Programs you like may not have high ratings, and your support could help keep them on the air. If you feel a commercial is inaccurate or misleading, write down the product, channel, time when you saw the commercial, and a brief description of your concern. Then call your local Better Business Bureau with the information, or send it to the Children's Advertising Review Unit, Council of Better Business Bureaus, Inc., 845 Third Avenue, New York, NY 10022.

Get help. Help is available. First, talk to your pediatrician or notify the American Academy of Pediatrics, P.O. Box 927, Elk Grove Village, IL 60009-0927 (708-228-5005). Additionally, many local parent-teacher associations (PTAs) and public service groups publish newsletters that review programs and describe activities to make television more beneficial. Action for Children's Television, or ACT (20 University Road, Cambridge, MA 02138), has been the leading public interest group. The parents of your children's friends and classmates can be useful allies. If you can get together with other parents and agree to enforce similar rules about the amount of TV watching and about what sorts of programs are suitable, you can avoid some of the intense peer pressure that makes it difficult for your children to follow your viewing suggestions.

Most important, end your passivity about television. Be assertive. Television is more than a way of eliminating boredom. It frequently acts like an uninvited guest, teaching your children lessons you do not suspect. It is essential that you know what your children are watching and help them to understand and learn from what they see.

For a variety of reasons, it may be difficult for parents to effectively monitor and control the amount of television their children watch. One solution is an electronic device that allows parents to automatically regulate the amount of television their children watch.

Viewing guidelines can be set in three different ways:

Daily scheduled viewing allows you to program the times of the day (or night) that your child is allowed to watch television. You can set two scheduled viewing intervals per day. For example, you may want to set a scheduled viewing interval so that your child can watch an educational show before school from 7 A.M. to 8 A.M., then set a second scheduled viewing interval for afternoon viewing between 4 P.M. and 5:30 P.M. These scheduled intervals are completely flexible, and each day of the week may be set up differently to suit the needs of the individual child.

Daily viewing allowance allows you to establish a set amount of time that is the total amount of television your child will be able to watch during that day. This daily allowance can be anywhere from 15 minutes to 24 hours. Different allowances can be set for each day of the week.

Weekly viewing allowance allows you to establish a set number of hours that is the total amount of television your child will be able to watch during any given week.

This sort of device allows parents to create a flexible and tailored viewing guideline. For example, you may have a child who does not need to have daily scheduled viewing times but does need to have a daily allowance assigned. In this case the child would be allowed to watch any time of the day but could not exceed the daily viewing allowance. Or you might want to set up the daily scheduled viewing so there is no television after 9 P.M. Such monitoring not only solves the problem of unchecked and excessive television viewing but can teach your children to budget their viewing time and to select quality programming instead of spending mindless hours in front of the TV.

This can also be used to limit the use of video games and VCRs as well. If you have video tapes in your home library that are not suitable for viewing by younger children or if you are concerned that your child may rent and view an inappropriate tape while you are away from home, then you can stop TV use until you are present.

Do Your Children Really Know How Much You Love Them?

"It's amazing," lamented fourteen-year-old Audrey. "Only four months old, and Ashley gets all the attention. I have to beg and plead for three days to get my parents to come see me in the class play, and all that kid has to do to get attention is spit up and smile!" Audrey, like most children, equated her parents' attention with love.

You know you would overcome more obstacles and face more barriers than Indiana Jones ever dreamed of in order to be there for your children, but do *they* know that? Do they feel your committed dedication? Do your children know you will always be there for them, no matter what, or do they believe your love has strings attached? Small children might feel that if they are naughty, Mommy and Daddy won't love them anymore. Few people can resist a cooing baby. Toddlers in their dumpy rompers are adorable. How adorable is a fifteen-year-old with impossible hair, a bad complexion, weird clothes, and an attitude problem?

Older Children May Feel Their Parents Love Them Less

Though your older children may need less physical attention, they still need to feel loved. Just because your adolescent daughter doesn't run across the room for a hug, jump into your lap, or wait at the window for you to come home doesn't mean she wants to be ignored. With some teenagers, you're acknowledged not as the source of hugs and kisses but as the keeper of the car keys. When we treat adolescents as smaller versions of adults or leave them to themselves, teens interpret this new aloneness not as freedom but as rejection. They begin to believe that their parents don't love them anymore, or don't love them as much as before. Even adolescents who are struggling to gain a measure of independence, to be their own person, don't want to be left alone.

Do your children feel the depth of your love for them? The key is communication. Words can be empowering and give your children the knowledge that you love them even more now than you did when they were little. Are you talking about your love, or are you talking *at* your children? Does your communication run along the lines of "Take out the trash," "Don't pick on your little sister," "You watch that attitude"?

Creating a Better Bond with Your Children

What are you doing to help your children feel connected to you? A busy parent sometimes needs to be creative. My daughter, a tremendous athlete, goes from one sports season to the next. I sometimes go up to school just to watch her in practice sessions. Why? Because even though I can't always make all of her regular games, I know the most important connection is for her to feel that I'm interested in her, not just whether the team wins. My being there at these practice times represents interest in *her.* She doesn't have to be a star to get my attention. I make it clear to her that *she's* worthwhile. I need to show her that while I'm a busy person, she counts in my life.

How can you show your children that you love them and need and want a wonderful relationship? Only you know what works with a particular child, but here are the basics.

Talk about your bond. How are the two of you doing? In what areas does your child want more attention? In what ways have the two of you created *inter*dependence? Ask, "Of all the things going on in your life, what's most important to you right now? How's it going? How can I be of help?" Before the response, see if you know what your child will say. Are your responses the same?

Participate in your child's life. How much you participate in your child's life tells how important your child is to you. If you don't feel you are participating enough in your child's life, your child probably has the same idea. But you can turn this around. A little honesty is a good place to start. "Chris, I have been so busy lately I haven't made time to follow you in Little League. And I miss it. I enjoy being with you, and I have fun every time we're together. I'm going to come to your game tonight and put next week's game on my calendar and not let anything get in the way of my being there."

Keep commitments. Children build their hopes around your promises. Your children need to learn that they can trust you to keep your word, even when doing so may be inconvenient. You expect your children to keep their word to you; just because you're an adult does not mean you shouldn't have to keep yours to them.

Demonstrate your love. You can't simply assume your children know you love them; you must show your love. Don't say, "Of course I love you; I'm your mother, aren't I?" Children want to know that you love them because they're worth loving, not because parents are supposed to love their children. They want to feel it. There are many different ways in which you can express this love, verbally or nonverbally.

You can just tell your children you love them. Say the words directly, don't hint at them. There's no need to be coy or cute, or to worry that you'll embarrass them (as long as you don't get mushy in front of their friends). Say "I love you, you mean everything to me" as often as you feel it. Make remarks such as "You're a wonderful son, Bill," "Have a good time, Joan, and take care of yourself for me," "You're so important to me, Roger," or "I like to be with you, Mary Louise." These are significant statements to our children, because from these remarks children draw conclusions about how connected they are to us and get an idea of how that feels to us.

Nonverbal expressions are as important as what you say. Your facial expression and body language communicate your love and bonding to your child almost as directly as your words do. Even newborns can sense our love and acceptance of them. Touching, for example, is a very powerful way of showing your feelings of love and acceptance. Taking your son's hand, patting him on the back, stroking his hair, straightening a collar, or simply touching his arm all express your love and pride in him. Several years ago I was in my office talking with colleagues when my daughter, then twelve years old, walked in from a candy run to the campus bookstore. While continuing my conversation with my colleagues, I put my arm around her, drawing her into the circle of adults. She never forgot it and will still bring that moment up.

Show acceptance. Accept your children for who they are. Your little girl is not a younger version of you or a clone of her sister. She is herself and wants to be accepted for her own strengths and weaknesses. When you show that acceptance, your children know you recognize them for themselves.

Tell your children they are special. I say to my daughter, "You are so important to me, Jennifer," followed by *here's why* statements. "I enjoy your friendship so much," or "I can always count on your support," or "You make me feel so happy and proud that you are my daughter." Such statements are more meaningful than the overused, "I love you." (But if you rarely tell your children "I love you," by all means say that!)

Talk about why you're happy to be a parent. Don't give your children the feeling that they are burdens, or that you're stuck with them. Remember, they'll live up to your expectations. You want them to feel special, worthy, able to stand up and be counted. "Jennifer, I love being your mother because you are such a loving daughter. Parenting you has been one of my greatest joys. It has been fun to watch you grow, and to watch you learn how to do things. I have really enjoyed loving you, and getting to know you inside, and learning what is important to you."

Do You Say "I Like You" as Often as "I Love You"?

How do you communicate with your children? What language do you use? Do you give encouragement, showing love with all that you say? Do you tell your children how important they are to you, how much you not only love them but like and respect them as well? The messages you send your children help them decide how valuable and worthwhile they are.

Use positive language. An unavoidable part of parenting is correcting our children. Yet even criticism can be given in a positive, lighthearted, even humorous manner. For example, "You did a great job cleaning up your room. I like how you put everything neatly on the shelf; that looks very nice. Maybe next time you could dust the shelf first to make it look even better." Or, "Thanks for taking the message from my boss, son. It was very important to me, and I appreciate your taking it all down; I know it was long. Please let me know next time as soon as I come home, rather than telling me hours later. If you do that for me, I promise I'll tell you right away the next time you get a call."

Insist that your children use positive language. When you hear your children talking about themselves, encourage them to use positive language. If your daughter says, "I'm so fat I look like Tubby the Tuba!" you can remind her that she hurts herself by putting herself down with such zingers. The two of you together can change her defeating language to encouraging language. "If I eat just one candy instead of several, my weight will start to drop and I'll look even better." Discourage negative self-talk.

Teach your children to receive and give compliments. Even very young children need to know how to accept a compliment gracefully. How many times have you told your son he looked cute, only to hear a surly snarl in reply, "Oh great, cute! That's just the image I want the guys on the team to have of me! Cute—geesh!" How much nicer it would be if he would say, "Cute? Well, that's a new one. I was shooting for handsome or even cool, but thanks." Children are more likely to give compliments when they get them themselves. If you regularly praise your children, even for little things, if you let them know you are happy with them, proud of them, they feel good about themselves and are likely to share that good feeling with others. A child who hears regularly how smart she is will be able to say to her friend, "Nice job on that spelling test; you got the hard one I missed." The child who is criticized is going to be envious and small minded, begrudging her friends their successes.

Compliment your children. We often boast about our children to others; they need to hear the good news themselves.

"Jack, I'm impressed with how you buckled down this semester and got your math grade up. And this extra-credit assignment you did is the icing on the cake. Good job!" "Sheila, I noticed how patient you were with your little sister when you were helping her clean up her room. You're a really good sister. Even though she may not say it or show it, I know she appreciates you as much as your father and I do."

Criticize the *action*, not the *child*. You're not upset with your children; you're upset with what they've done. Make that clear in your criticism. "Chad, you didn't make your bed this morning. I want you to make it every morning without my having to tell you each time." How much kinder and more to the point this is than bellowing, "Chad! Get in here! How many times, how many many times, do I have to tell you to make your bed? Why don't you listen to me? When are you going to grow up and assume some responsibility?" With the critical comment, Chad doesn't hear the problem—the unmade bed—but only the disappointment that his parent has in him. He hears not that he has left an unmade bed, a small problem in the scheme of things, but that he is irresponsible and immature.

Let old wrongs remain in the past. Sometimes we adults have an unfortunate habit of repeating ourselves, thinking we are making a point. "That's the seventh time this month you've smarted back to me." "I've told you every day this week to take out the trash." "You're doing it again. This is just like that time last summer when I told you you couldn't go to the party and you went behind my back." If your children hear this from you constantly, what motivation do they have to right a wrong? They're going to hear about that wrong forever, no matter what. They hear not love and encouragement from you but score-keeping.

Set positive expectations and believe in your child. If you want your children to know how much you love them, let them know what you expect of them and that your expectations are positive. A boy needs to hear, "I know you can get a B in English if you read those books and do the reports the way your teacher showed you." The child then knows that you believe in him. What does he feel if he hears you saying, "And I don't want you to shirk mowing the lawn this week as you did last Saturday!" All he can think of then is that since you already expect the worst, he has nothing to lose by giving you what you expect.

Apologize when you are wrong. Adults too often feel that because they set the rules they don't have to apologize for breaking them. We have the same responsibilities to our children as we do to our adult friends, to our spouses, to our coworkers. If you're wrong, say so and make amends.

Listen emphatically. Listen not with just your ears but with your mind and heart. You listen emphatically when you try to understand the whole communication, the body language, the tone, the hidden meanings. You seek to understand your children's point of view, then express how you feel about it. "I hear you saying . . . " "I believe you are telling me . . . " "I feel that . . . " You make "I" statements, which own your words, rather than "you" statements ("You are stubborn . . . " "You are overreacting"), which create defensiveness. Listening is really a matter of acceptance. When you listen, you make it clear that you care about your children. You make an effort to see things from their point of view, realizing that it is as real and right to them as your point of view is to you. You don't have to agree with everything your children say; don't be afraid to let them know when you do disagree. But let them know you are listening, and they will know that you care for and respect them. They will know they are emotionally secure in your love.

Give gold stars. Remember when the actress Sally Field claimed an Oscar award and babbled, "You like me! You really like me!" People teased her about her outburst, but it came from the heart. We all need to feel liked. Until we know others like us, we cannot truly be secure. Do your children know how much you like them? Teachers at school give children gold stars on their papers to show they've done a good job. Are you giving your children enough gold stars at home, praising them and showing them how much you appreciate them?

Helping our children feel secure in our love is a conscious decision on our part. When children know that they are loved and cherished, and live in an environment where love is supremely valued, they experience the true meaning of inner happiness. They are also more likely to create an environment conducive to a healthy and nourishing emotional life when they raise their own families.

8

Why Is Self-Esteem Important?

Have you ever wondered why some children radiate happiness and seem to be more self-confident than others? Have you ever noticed how some kids believe they are pretty important and valuable, while others don't seem to think very much of themselves? One reason for these differences is the value we assign to our being, our personhood, our life. That's the power of self-esteem. Self-esteem contributes to your child's happiness and emotional well-being. We hear so much about self-esteem. What is it, and how does it contribute to your child's overall well-being?

What Is Self-Esteem?

Self-esteem is self-regard. It's the esteem you hold for you, the value you place on your personhood. Self-esteem is a self-picture, the reputation you hold for yourself. It becomes your price tag, so to speak. What's *your* children's price tag? Does it read VALUABLE MERCHANDISE? MARKDOWN? REJECT? Self-esteem can determine the level of joy, satisfaction, energy, and commitment your children bring to living their lives fully.

Your Children's Self-Esteem Determines Their Inner Wellness

The picture children have of themselves is a key to their self-esteem. Self-concept is so important that it permeates all of life. How children feel about themselves affects how they grow, how well they learn, how they get along with friends, how strongly they are motivated to try new tasks. It sets the tone of interaction in the parent-child relationship and may even influence how much you enjoy parenting. Self-esteem can determine how well children do in school, the goals they set and achieve, and how much potential they develop. A child's inner picture is vitally important. Whether this picture is accurate or inaccurate, healthy or dysfunctional, actions flow from this inner picture of self-worth. This is why children who see themselves in a positive light act positively; children who see themselves as problems are usually in trouble. A student's self-perception becomes the baseline for performance in school. The level of a child's self-esteem will empower or detract from the child's happiness and well-being. The level of a child's self-esteem will contribute to how that child experiences life.

The following simple little story about the boy who came home from school crying illustrates just how important self-perception is.

"Why are you crying, Paul?" his grandmother asked.

"Because Fred called me a sissy. Do you think I'm a sissy, Grandma?"

"Oh, no," said the grandmother. "I think you're a Ferrari."

"What?" said the boy, trying to make sense of what his grandmother had said. "Why do you think I'm a car?"

"Well, if you believe that because Fred called you a sissy, you are, you might as well believe you're a car. Why be a sissy when you can be a Ferrari?"

"Oh," exclaimed the boy gleefully, quite relieved. "*I* get to decide what I am!"

And that is, in effect, what we want to help our children believe. Why be a sissy when you can be a Ferrari? Unfortunately, and all too often, a young person like Paul believes his personal price tag reads DAMAGED GOODS instead of VALUABLE MERCHANDISE. Children who have been hurt or abandoned by those they love underestimate themselves, and often exaggerate their self-worth as a way of compensating for low self-esteem.

How Do You Build a Healthy and Durable Sense of Self?

You don't just wake up one day with bad self-esteem or good self-esteem, with high self-esteem or low self-esteem. It's developed over time. You *earn* your self-esteem. Healthy self-esteem is best achieved by actively participating in life in a meaningful way. You are willing to be your own best friend, to live life fully and with zest, to stand up for yourself in all encounters, in good times and bad, to take responsibility for the choices you make, your actions, and your behavior. You work toward those things that are important to you. You want to live your life in a meaningful and purposeful way.

The Six Ingredients of Self-Esteem

Over the years and around the globe my work with youth, parents, educators, researchers, and child-care practitioners has led me to discover that there are six key areas in which self-esteem is empowered or eroded. Our experiences, positive and negative, in each of these areas contribute to or detract from the level of our self-esteem. For youth, these six are both developed and eroded in hierarchical order. Positive experiences in these areas build a positive sense of self, while negative experiences in one or more of these areas seriously erodes a child's self-esteem. The six vital ingredients of self-esteem are:

- physical safety (freedom from physical harm)
- emotional security (the absence of intimidations and fears)
- identity (the "Who am I?" question)
- affiliation (a sense of belonging)
- competence (how capable one feels) and
- mission (the feeling that one's life has meaning and direction).

Throughout the years of childhood, these six powerful ingredients of self-esteem are largely influenced by parents and educators. To a large degree we color, or set in motion, children's perception of themselves. We can see readily the effects of these six elements at work:

1. Physical safety: Children who feel physically safe aren't fearful of being harmed or hurt. They feel safe in the home, school, and neighborhood. They care about their health, knowing they must not put it in jeopardy and must protect themselves from danger. Because they feel safe and know how to be safe, they learn to be open and to trust others. They freely exercise a curious nature (this will contribute to learning). They move about with a sense of healthy assuredness. Their body posture displays confidence. Their tone of voice is hearty, and they will maintain eye contact when talking with you.

2. Emotional security: Children who know they won't be put down or made to feel unworthy, or be beaten up emotionally with sarcasm or hurtful words, develop a high level of emotional security. Because they feel emotionally secure, they learn to be caring and compassionate with themselves and others. They become trustworthy. They feel secure in sharing opinions and ideas. They are respectful and considerate, outgoing and friendly. They will come to you for hugs of affection, reach out to touch, enjoy being close to you. They like to snuggle.

3. Identity: Children with self-knowledge develop a healthy sense of individuality. They know themselves. They are friends with the face in the mirror. They can "knock and find somebody home." They believe in their worth as human beings. Believing they are worthy of praise, they feel secure in praising and complimenting others. Feeling secure, they are open and caring toward others. They take responsibility for their actions and will own up to them.

4. Belonging: Children who feel accepted by and connected to others feel liked, appreciated, and respected. They learn to seek out and maintain friendships. They are able to cooperate and share. While maintaining a sense of independence, they learn *inter*dependence, a healthy interrelatedness.

5. Competence: When youngsters feel they are good at some things, they are willing to learn how to do other things. Because they feel capable, they are willing to persevere rather than give up when things become difficult. They are not only aware of their strengths but are able to accept areas of less ability, without developing "victim" behavior. Because they try, they experience successes that encourage them to try new things. They are self-empowered through realistic and achievable goals and therefore have initiative.

6. Purpose: Children with a strong sense of mission feel purposeful. Life has meaning. Because they have a sense of direction, they not only sets goals but follow through on achieving them. They have identified their values and live accordingly. Their values are reflected in their behavior; their actions are a reflection of their values. They have an inner knowledge, an inner peace. They are intuitive. They laugh easily. They are joyful.

A healthy self-esteem does not promote conceit or self-centeredness but, rather, gives children a realistic awareness of themselves and of their abilities and needs. With an all-encompassing self-respect, those children are unwilling to allow others to devalue their worth, nor will they let others deprive them of their needs. They are less likely to squander their talents and aptitudes, be it through procrastination, substance use, or other means. They care about themselves.

We Wear Our Self-Esteem

We wear our self-esteem like a suit of clothes. Because self-regard is reflected in our behavior, other people can see what we think of ourselves. The way we communicate—our choice of words, how well we listen, our style of relating to others—are just a few of the many telltale signs of how we value ourselves. Another telltale sign is who we hang out with, our choice of friends.

Every Child Needs a Healthy Self-Esteem

All children need a positive sense of self-worth and a feeling of being OK. Remember that behavior is a direct result of a child's feelings of worth and value. That's why behavior is such a telltale sign of how children feel about themselves. Bad behavior is often a sign that something is wrong. School dropouts, early pregnancy, drug abuse, and other destructive behavior, for the most part, have a lot to do with a child's self-esteem, just as does school performance. I have never heard of a child who was asked to leave a school because of an inability to learn. A dropout is a child who sees little purpose to life, has a difficult time relating school success to the outside world, and sees few reasons to try to improve. Such a child also has difficulty developing warm relationships with peers and teachers— the support system that makes school a fun and endurable place. These negative behaviors and feelings are a direct result of a damaged sense of self. The need for a positive self-regard is evident.

Characteristics of Children with High Self-Esteem

- The higher children's self-esteem, the better able they are to cope with the ups and downs of life.
- The higher children's self-esteem, the more apt they are to attract others who have high self-esteem. Children with low self-esteem seek other children who think poorly of themselves. We are naturally drawn to others with a similar sense of self-regard.
- The higher children's self-esteem, the more likely they are to think about what they want out of life, go after it, and achieve it.

- The higher children's self-esteem, the more likely they are to treat others with respect; self-respect is the basis of respect for others.
- The higher children's self-esteem, the more secure they are in confronting obstacles, fears, and interpersonal conflicts rather than avoiding them, in solving problems instead of worrying over them. Children with low self-esteem see problems as grounds for quitting and often say to themselves, "I give up." Instead of comparing their achievements with their own goals and potential, they compare themselves with others and wait for others to create their "successes."
- The higher children's self-esteem, the better able they are to find ways to get along well with others and then respond positively to them. They strive to be useful, helpful, purposeful, and responsible.
- The higher children's self-esteem, the better able they are to find compassion for themselves and show compassion for others. Compassion exposes self-worth: They have discovered the treasured value of their personhood.
- The higher children's self-esteem, the more secure, decisive, friendly, trusting, cheerful, optimistic, and purposeful they are. Look closely and you'll also discover that they are motivated, or, as we say, "empowered." That's because they recognize their own worth and achievements without a constant need for approval from the outside.
- The higher children's self-esteem, the more responsibility and control they will take over their actions. This is very important, not only because children who monitor their own actions are responsible, but

because these children are more willing to accept challenges because they have experienced previous successes. Recognition of personal strengths and capabilities serves as a powerful coping and buffer strategy for overcoming obstacles and helps compensate for weaknesses and setbacks.

- The higher children's self-esteem, the more resilient they are to problems and defeats.
- The higher children's self-esteem, the more content and self-fulfilled they are.
- One of the joys of parenting is seeing our children become confident, emotionally secure, happy, and self-accepting individuals. When we teach our children that they get to choose whether they will be a Ferrari or a sissy, we teach them the important lesson of self-efficacy and self-respect.

How to Help Your Children Gain a Healthy Identity

Sometimes a child's inner picture needs only minor repair, sometimes it needs to be fine-tuned or refocused, and sometimes it needs to be replaced by an entirely new picture. You can help your child construct a healthy identity and even repair a bruised one. Ensuring that your children's self-esteem is sound and healthy has to do with the six vital ingredients. A good many suggestions for developing self-esteem are provided throughout this book. In a nutshell, they are:

- Keep your children physically safe.
- Be careful not to tear your children down. Avoid using sarcasm, don't swear, and don't always focus on what your children aren't doing well; instead, catch

your children doing things right and, when they do, acknowledge them.

- Let your children know that you are supportive of them, that you are in their camp, and that your love is unconditional. While you may not always be supportive of certain of their actions, you believe in their basic and inherent goodness.

- Provide your children with a sense of self-knowledge, of knowing who they are. Help them puzzle out their place in the world and discuss the importance of living life in an aware fashion, that we must each be personally and socially responsible.

- Help your children feel capable. Help them learn how to set and achieve goals, to value achievement, and to recognize their own innate interests and talents.

- Help your children internalize their value and see life as something to be cherished, lived to the fullest in a responsible fashion.

Help Your Children Build a Positive Sense of Identity

Children want to be individuals, not just "Mike's son" or "Eileen's daughter." Developing this individual identity is vital in developing and maintaining strong mental health, in keeping safe and secure emotionally. Children who are emotionally safe know who they are, and where they fit into the overall scheme of things vis-à-vis their families, their neighborhoods, their schools. Older children need to know their roles in ever-increasing circles, including the world in general. All children at some point wrestle with the question, "Who am I?" Yet children often hide themselves until they feel secure in letting the "real me" show. The poem "The Paint Brush" by Lee Ezell says it best.

I keep my paint brush with me
Wherever I may go,
In case I need to cover up
So the real me doesn't show.
I'm so afraid to show you me,
Afraid of what you'll do.
You might laugh or say mean things;
I'm afraid I might lose you.
I'd like to remove all of my paint coats
To show you the real, true me,
But I want you to try and understand
I need you to like what you see.
So if you'll be patient and close your eyes
I'll strip off all my coats real slow,
Please understand how much it hurts
To let the real me show.
Now my coats are all stripped off
I feel naked, bare and cold,
If you still love me with all that you see
You are my friend pure as gold.
I need to save my paint brush though
And hold it in my hand,
I want to keep it handy
In case somebody don't understand.
So please protect me, my dear friend,
And thanks for loving me true,
But please let me keep my paint brush with me
Until I love me, too.

You can help your children develop a healthy self-description. You'll want to start by getting a sense of how they see themselves. Ask questions. "What four words best describe you? How do you see yourself? What four words best describe how you would *like* to be? How do you think others see you? If they were to describe you, what would they say?"

The Importance of Appearance

Children spend a good deal of time talking about themselves in relation to other children. Much of that will be based on appearance.

At quite an early age, a child begins to form a concept of self and others based on outer beauty, and to differentiate between what the child considers to be attractive and unattractive. You may say, "It's what's inside that counts," but to a child, appearance and physical features are an important part of identity (as is hairstyle). This awareness begins as early as three years of age, when children stereotype others on the basis of physical attractiveness. Attractive children are looked at, smiled at, touched, and asked to play more often than other children. Attractive children are also named as best friends more often than other children.

Studies on the psychology of teaching show that teachers call on attractive children more often than unattractive children. Teachers define attractive as a generally neat and clean appearance. An attractive child has parents who pay attention to the child's clothes, who bathe and fuss over the child, and perhaps match a ribbon or socks to the child's attire. These children receive the most positive numbers of eye contacts by teachers, and they garner the most positive strokes, or reinforcements, in the classroom as well. This means that such children receive a good share of positive attention, a plus in helping them cope with the normal frustrations of learning and, of course, in feeling good about themselves. These very attributes—positive attention, stroking, touching, and verbal and non-verbal affirmations—are factors that contribute to helping a child become an overachiever or underachiever.

Clothes do count. Children who do not dress like the other children, and that includes those who are over-dressed as well as poorly dressed, feel different and have negative feelings about themselves. That's why so many private schools request that students wear a uniform and why some public schools have dress codes. Dressing alike puts students on an equal footing.

Just as you have an acceptable standard of dress at your place of work, so do your children. Are you familiar with school clothing? You should ask these questions:

- When was the last time I observed each of my children at school with their peers?
- How does their overall appearance compare with other classmates?
- How do my children look in relationship to their peers?
- Are my children clean and well groomed each day?
- Have I imposed restrictions that are unfair?
- Are my children overdressed?
- How do my children feel about their appearance?
- How would my children say others describe their appearance?

Making sure a child looks like other children doesn't have to mean a big emphasis on clothes but, rather, seeing to it that your children are neat and clean and feel good about their appearance. After that, reassure your children that they don't need exciting packaging to be loved and accepted. You want to help them accept themselves—to gain a greater sense of personhood in a realistic, self–assuring way and not to have all of their self–perceptions come from their physical being.

The Importance of Friends

The child's first self-perceptions come from you, from a reflection in your eyes. If you believe a child is well-mannered, intelligent and capable and say so, the child believes it too. All children need to feel special, especially to their parents.

Interactions with other children provide your child with another view of this unique identity. The first questions children ask as they enter a new classroom or new situation have little to do with teachers or the academic curriculum. They ask, "Who is in my class?" "Who will I sit next to?" "What are their names?" "Will they like me?" Social acceptance dominates their thinking. The need to belong can cause enormous stress, particularly if a child is not considered to be one of the group, yet many children go through school with few friends, and many are without friends entirely.

Why do you think that's so? It's because peers, for the most part, are situational friends. You might be my friend because we're neighbors, or because we share a locker or a class together, are on the same team, or get assigned to do a special project. But these friendships rarely last very long. Indeed, some don't even survive a few months. Nearly 37 percent of elementary school children are not named as a friend by anyone in their class, and 29 percent receive no nomination from anyone in the school setting. They get even fewer votes as they get older.

You can't always be there to assist your children in their relationships with other people, but you can do some things to help your children develop the skills they need to make and sustain friendships.

Help your child understand the nature of friendships. Children who understand the simple psychology of interactions with their peers, will feel more confident about their ability to relate successfully to others without feeling that they are abandoned because they are unlovable or unworthy of their company when the friendship changes or falls apart.

Help each child examine the nature of friendships and the influence friends have. You may want to refer to the Suggested Reading section at the back of this book for resources, or ask your child's teacher or local public librarian for a recommended reading list designed with the age of the child in mind.

Encourage your children to invite friends over. Children from homes where parents allow other children to come and visit are candidates for being popular with their friends. A place to hang out is one requirement of friendship. You may want to encourage your child to invite other children over, but only when you are there to supervise.

Make your home more inviting. If your child doesn't want others to come over, it may be because of embarrassment about something in the home. "My sister throws her underwear in a laundry basket in the hallway where you enter the house. No way will I take the chance that my friends will see it," said sixteen-year-old Thomas. When I was in high school, there was one particular boy I wanted to date. He was, as Bart Simpson would say, "a real cool dude." But I was embarrassed by the way our screen door looked, tattered from six children opening and closing it over the years. You know what? I turned that boy down for every date he ever asked for! There was no way I was about to let such a guy see that door. Yet if I had told my parents I was dateless for the prom because of that screen door, they would have thought me silly. Ask your child about your home. There's a good possibility that a few complaints, like that laundry basket in the wrong spot, can be rectified.

A strong and positive sense of identity is a sign of emotional strength. Children who feel emotionally safe in their families and in their relationships are able to develop and respect their own individuality.

We help our children to develop a positive self-regard when we make it clear to them that we not only love them but respect and like them as well. The emotional security of knowing that the most important people in their lives, their parents, cherish them will remain with your children forever.

IV

*Keeping Your Children Safe
Spiritually*

9

Six Universal Truths to Teach Your Children

As parents, we hope with all our hearts that we are able to keep our children safe. One dimension of wellness is providing a spiritual base, to love from and be loved by. This is our responsibility to God and to our children.

We keep our children spiritually safe when we impart our love of God to them, to show not only that *we* love them but that there is a Higher Power who loves them too and provides an all-empowering love. Keeping our children safe spiritually means transmitting values for spiritual truths that provide a solid foundation which our children can build their lives on and use to sustain them in their lifetime journey. This power base can nourish and provide them with the strength and courage to live a meaningful, joyful, and productive life. We must lovingly endow our children with a desire to experience God's love.

What Principles Must We Teach?

Convincing our children to embrace the ideals necessary for nourishing their spiritual lives is relatively simple. Helping them to live by these time-honored truths is a more difficult parenting challenge. Teaching a young child how to pray each evening, for example, is easy in comparison to convincing a teenager to seek God's advice, when pressured by peers to drink or do drugs, and to call upon God's strength in not yielding to peer pressure in belittling, teasing, or threatening others.

So how do we keep our children spiritually safe? What shall we do? How shall we do it? Where does a parent begin? Turning our hearts heavenward in seeking direction is a good beginning, for our mission is great: We must teach our children to love God, to love themselves, and to love their fellow beings. And they must come to understand this task as the overall mission and purpose of their lives.

One: A Relationship with God Is Important

The first spiritual truth is that a relationship with God is important. All major religions share a belief in the existence and oneness of God. In his book *Oneness: Great Principles Shared by All Religions* (pp. 12–13), Jeffrey Moses points this out by sharing what various faiths hold true.

> *Christianity teaches, "There is one God and Father of all, who is above all, and through all, and in you all."*
>
> *Judaism teaches, "Have we not all one Father? Has not one God created us?"*
>
> *Hinduism teaches, "He is the one God hidden in all beings, all-pervading, the Self within all beings, watching over all worlds, dwelling in all beings, the witness, the perceiver."*

Confucianism teaches, "Remember even when alone that the Divine is everywhere."

Sikhism teaches, "There is but one God whose name is true. He is the creator, immortal, self-existent."

How Do You Teach Your Children That God Exists?

Children who are small will accept nearly anything because Mommy or Daddy says it is so. To the very young, understanding God is no more momentous than learning where babies come from or why birds fly when they themselves cannot. As parents, our task is to use this time of acceptance to begin laying a foundation that will grow into an ever-stronger faith that can survive the normal questioning and challenges of our children's later years. If that hasn't been done, the task is to instill faith in a way for the child to embrace it now. Here are some of the ways we may help our children learn that God exists and that a relationship with God is important.

By responding to their curiosity. Children are by nature so inquisitive that the explanation of God's existence becomes required in its own time anyway. What parent hasn't heard some variation of these questions: "Where did the sun come from, Mommy?" "How did the world get here?" "Who made the ocean? the stars? the sky?" "Where do babies come from?" "What happens after you die?" Then, as children grow older: "Why do bad things happen to good people?" "What does God have to do with my life?" "If God is real, why doesn't God stop all the child abuse, murders, pollution, and suffering?" "Why can't we see, touch, and talk to God in person?" These and similar questions provide great opportunities for telling your child about the existence of this great and loving Spirit and about the importance of a relationship with God.

Through illustration. In the hand of God "is the life of every living thing and the breath of all mankind" (Job 12:10). God's existence is evident all around us. Talk about obvious miracles of creation; all creation points to God.

- The fascinating habits of animals on the ground or in the air, which are dangerous and which aren't, and how God gave those "dangers" to animals for their protection
- The intricacy and beauty in the colors and shapes and fragrances of flowers; how the bees fly to them to gather their pollen
- The changing of the seasons
- The mystery of migration, why birds can fly, and how some can also swim
- The assortment of seashells on the beach—differing sizes, shapes, colors, and patterns—and how little sea creatures make in them homes
- The magnificence of the ocean, with its crashing waves, that stretches over the globe; the changing of the tides
- Billions of stars—more than we could ever count—sparkling thousand of miles away in the night sky
- The sun with its endless power and brilliance to warm and give light
- The many races, distinctions, and abilities of human beings

Regardless of your children's ages, you will find many opportunities to note how many wonders God has created. With very small children, you could take a walk and talk about—literally!—the birds and the bees and the various other flora and fauna you see during your stroll. With older children, you might encourage them to think about the incredible intricacies of the world they are learning about in school, how there must be a God to have created such a wonderful, complicated machine as the human body and a system so efficient as nature.

Helping your children be aware of just how great and endless God's creation is will reinforce the belief that God exists, and the importance of a relationship with God becomes obvious.

By reading. Perhaps you take your children to Sunday school to learn about the presence of God in our lives. How about in your home? Are there reading materials to help your children expand their awareness? Have you taught the use of prayer materials and religious texts, to seek, to knock, to connect with God? Do your children see you reading in your quest to expand your spiritual knowledge?

By example. As a parent, you are probably the most important role model in your children's lives. Your values and beliefs become theirs. Every time your children see you praying or asking for guidance or reading your Bible, they receive the message that you accept God's existence, that you believe a relationship with God is important, and that this relationship greatly enriches your life.

By increasing your knowledge base. If you want your children to believe that God exists and that a relationship with God is important, you need to impart this message continually, by your actions as well as by your words. One important action is seeking to broaden and deepen your own understanding of the graces of God. Spiritual bookstores offer a wide variety of books, audio cassettes, and videos. You can attend lectures and seminars or go to group meetings at your church or temple. Let your children see you trying to enlarge your own knowledge, seeing that you want to learn more. Teenagers, especially, need to know that you are committed to this quest, that faith is not something merely for younger children. This is especially true for older, more jaded and cynical children who have been victims of a series of negative or destructive experiences, who need not only a foundation of faith but first-hand experience of how God's grace applies to their lives every day and always.

Two: God Is a Loving Creator

Equally important as teaching your children about the existence of God is teaching them about God's love for them—that God is a loving creator. Again, this belief is shared by essentially every faith (Moses, *Oneness*, pp. 104–105).

> *Christianity teaches, "God is love, and he who abides in love abides in God, and God abides in him."*
> *Buddhism teaches, "He that loveth not, knoweth not God. For God is love."*
> *Judaism teaches, "Love is the beginning and end of the Torah."*

Children are extremely receptive, both to our love and to God's love. We want our children to believe that God's plan is to love them always, in good times and bad. This assurance gives children a source of strength to carry them through difficult or painful experiences as they grow up.

When Fran was a young girl, her parents told her frequently, "God loves you." As is typical with a young child, Fran would smile and keep on playing. Acceptance was axiomatic. As Fran grew older, however, she found her faith challenged on many occasions. She would doubt whether a loving God could cause her to go through problems, both small (lack of acceptance by the kids at a new school, inability to make the cheerleading squad) and large (losing a good friend during the war, having another friend lose a limb in a car accident), but she always reminded herself that faith in God and God's unconditional love for her would help her through these painful experiences.

The most severe test of faith came when Fran was sixty, when she learned that her only son, Ron, was dying of AIDS. Her immediate panic sent her to prayer. At first she prayed for her son's recovery. When it was apparent that Ron was going to die she became angry, believing that a just God would not take her only son and certainly would not make him suffer through this dreadful, painful disease. The anger lasted a long time, until Ron's last few days. During that time, Fran spoke often with her grown son, uncertain whether he, drugged with morphine to ease the pain, could hear her. She heard herself telling him the same things she had taught him as a child: God loves you, God's plan is for the best even if we don't understand it, God's love will sustain us. As she talked, Fran felt herself calming down, accepting her son's death as part of his life's experience. She knew that God loved Ron and that God loved her and the rest of their family and would be with them as they dealt with this experience. Fran heard her own mother's words again as clearly as she had heard them when she was a child herself, as clearly as she had heard them throughout her teenage years and early married life, when times were especially difficult. She began to *know* at a deeper level that God was listening to her grief and anger about the suffering and loss of her son and that God, too, might be feeling anger and grief at the tragedy in their lives.

Fran reaffirmed her faith in God and was sustained by the knowledge and assurance of God's love. She found herself during her prayers thanking God for a mother and father who had given her the foundation of strength that saw her through this most difficult time in her life.

The belief that God loves and sustains us throughout all the experiences in our lives, all challenges, and in times of anguish is a powerful source of strength, as the following story, "Footprints" (author unknown), beautifully and poignantly illustrates.

One night a man had a dream. He dreamed he was walking down the beach with the Lord. Across the sky flashed scenes from his life. For most scenes, he noticed two sets of footprints in the sand: one belonging to him, and the other to the Lord.

When the last scene of his life flashed before him, he looked back at the footprints in the sand. He noticed that sometimes along the path of his life there was only one set of footprints. He also noticed that this happened at the very lowest and saddest times.

This really bothered him, and he questioned the Lord about it. "Lord, you said that once I decided to follow you, you'd walk with me all the way. But I noticed that during the most troublesome times in my life there is only one set of footprints. I don't understand why when I needed you most you would leave me."

The Lord replied, "My son, my precious child, I love you and I would never leave you. During your times of trial and suffering, when you see only one set of footprints, it was then that I carried you."

How Do You Teach Your Children About God's Love for Them?

Fran felt blessed that her parents had taught her of God's love for her. She hoped that she herself had been able to transmit the same comforting beliefs to her son. Because we accept that God's love is the most precious truth there is, we want to share that gift with our children. How can we do so, in a way that will be useful to our children and will cause them to call upon that strength rather than abandon it?

Explain it. Teach your children at an early age, by using simple terms and examples, that God loves them. Use stories and illustrations they can understand. Use examples that include their pets, friends, and family members, things they can relate to. Don't press your children with things that are too deep for them. By listening closely, you know whether your children can grasp what you are teaching. Ask the Holy Spirit to aid and give direction to your efforts to simplify great truths correctly and teach them effectively.

Reinforce God's love. Point out how loving it was of God to put those things that are wonderful in the world for every person to enjoy, not just nice people. When something particularly marvelous happens, let your children know it was a result of God's love. When some crisis is weathered, remind your children that God's love helped see them through. We don't always have to understand what is happening, we just need to believe God is for us and with us. Make God a part of everyday life, "for welfare and not for evil" (Jer. 29:11).

Exemplify it. Again, it is through your example that your children will learn and embrace spiritual values, from the most basic to those more complex. When you demonstrate your beliefs, when you are loving in an unconditional, all-forgiving way with your children, you are teaching them of God's divine love. When you guide with love and fairness, your children relate to your authority as they do to God's. Begin early; what you do in the early years becomes important in later years, when teens put spiritual faith to the test (their friends' and parents' as well as their own) as is shown by Nathan's challenge.

> Nathan's friend and classmate, John, a seventeen-year-old, was killed in a car accident. The two boys had been close friends since grade school. Nathan felt devastated and blamed God. He wanted to know why a loving God hadn't kept his friend safe? Nathan's questioning revealed his deep pain. "If there is a God," Nathan demanded, "why did God let John get killed? John didn't deserve to die. He was a good guy. He never did anything to hurt anybody."

> "Son, trust that John is with God," Nathan's father answered. "There are a lot of things I don't understand, but that doesn't change what I believe. God loves you, John, me. I know it's hard to comprehend John's death, but talk honestly with God about your feelings. God is big enough to help you handle your anger."

His father offered God as a source of comfort to Nathan and talked about how things happen that are hard to understand. Nathan didn't respond at that moment, but he took his father's words to his room with him, thinking of them and eventually finding comfort in them. By bridging the gap between his son's pain and his faith, Nathan's father was able to witness to his trust in a loving and wise God, provide understanding, and therefore help his son's faith survive this trial.

We can help our children learn to use God's love as a source of strength, too, and not see God as to blame for what we don't understand. If, for example, the accident was caused by a drunken or speeding driver, we can then talk about unacceptable human behavior and poor decision-making.

Teach forgiveness. We must also teach our children to believe in God's forgiveness. You teach your children this when you treat them with love and are willing to forgive their mistakes and shortcomings. Parents who are harsh with their children can make it more difficult for them to believe in a loving, forgiving heavenly parent. There are many Bible stories that tell of God's forgiveness of sinners; read these with your children and discuss everyday parallels.

Three: The Spirit of God Is Nurtured Within

Our children must learn that God must be nurtured within us. Children want to know, "Where is God?" "Where does God live?" "Where is heaven?" "Why can't I see God?" Teenagers have their own special set of questions: "Why is God so selective, seeming to help some people to have great lives and letting others suffer?" "Does God only like or exist for the people in certain countries?" "Why does God let so many people suffer and die?" "How can you say God is within someone who is criminal?" "What is a conscience?" Teach that God loves all people, though not all people love or honor God or want God in their lives. God abides in the people who want God. That God lives with each of us is another belief that is universal in its truth (Moses, *Oneness*, pp. 24–25).

Christianity teaches, "The kingdom of God is within you."
Hinduism teaches, "God bides hidden in the hearts of all."
Shintoism teaches, "Do not search the distant skies for God. In man's own heart is He found."
Sikhism teaches, "Even as the scent dwells within the flower, so God within thine own heart ever abides."

How Do You Teach Your Children That God Is in Them?

The Spirit of God lives in us, but we need to make the Spirit feel welcome and wanted, just as when we ask a friend to spend time with us. Part of instilling a strong faith in our children is letting them know that God is a part of their everyday lives, not just a powerful being discussed on Sunday mornings and turned to in times of crisis. We can help our children understand God's presence in our lives in several ways.

By discussing it. "But where does God live inside me?" your three-year-old might ask. You answer, "In your heart." Your six-year-old may be ready for a more detailed answer, "In that special place inside you that tells when you're doing something right or wrong; that makes you feel happy when you do something you know is right; that makes you content that you didn't do something you knew was wrong." Your answer will depend on you and your child and how much you feel your child is ready to learn and understand. For your sixteen-year-old, you might answer, "God is the very essence of each of us. You can recognize that truth by those powerful feelings that you can't help but feel when you've given your all, gone out of your way to help someone, or followed your conscience to do the right thing, even when you may have been tempted to follow another path. That recognized moment of wholeness, of goodness, adds to the proof of God within you."

God's promise to live in us if we want it and nurture it is, of course, the primary reason we know God lives in us. "Behold, I stand at the door and knock; if any one opens the door, I will come in" (Rev. 3:20).

By providing examples. Discuss with your children those times when they did something wrong but confessed their transgressions to God, you, their teachers, or the person they wronged, and felt a powerful sense of relief and strength for doing so. Remind them that our conscience is a way God reminds us of God's presence in us and love for us. God encourages us to do the right thing. Give examples of times when it would have been simple to take the easy way out or get away with something, but you (or they or their friends) made the extra effort, at some cost, to do the right thing. It is the God within them, within all of us, that helps us find the strength to do what we know is right. Our conscience is a gift from God; it is a guiding light. When aligned with God's true word, it tells us wrong from right.

By rejoicing in goodness. There are so many daily examples of people going out of their way to do something kind for others, even for strangers they may never see again. Discuss these examples, taking them from television viewing, from newspapers, from talks with your friends. Encourage your children to think about kind things that have been done for them. Why did someone act so nicely? Remind your children that God teaches us of the value of kindness and giving, that when we give to others we give to God and please God. It is the God within us that rejoices when we treat our brothers and sisters as ourselves.

Four: Loving Others Comes from a Good Relationship with God

A teapot filled with tea pours out tea; a person filled with love pours out love. God is love. Our love comes from God. This means that within us we have an almost infinite capacity for love. Love needs to be given to others, to be shared with those around us. We find the true meaning of spirituality when we give of ourselves. When your children are young, you teach them to share their toys. When your children are older, you encourage them to do community work, something to help others. Perhaps you yourself do volunteer work, to set an example. One of the most valuable things you can do is teach your children to share not only their possessions and their time but the vast reservoir of love within themselves, a principle basic to many faiths. (Moses, *Oneness,* pp. 4–5).

> *Christianity teaches, "Do unto others as you would have others do unto you."*
>
> *Islam teaches, "Do unto all men as you would wish to have done unto you; and reject for others what you would reject for yourselves."*
>
> *Judaism teaches, "What is hurtful to yourself do not to your fellow man."*
>
> *Buddhism teaches, "Hurt not others with that which pains yourself."*
>
> *Hinduism teaches, "This is the sum of all righteousness: Treat others, as thou wouldst thyself be treated."*
>
> *Confucianism teaches, "What you do not yourself desire, do not put before others."*

How Do You Teach Your Children to Love Others?

The parental paradox: When our children are little, we tell them not to talk to strangers. When our children are older, we tell them to be very careful of whom they associate with, whom they date. Yet at the same time we tell them to love and accept others, to recognize that everyone is unique, special, and worthy of love. How do we reconcile these seemingly disparate points of view? How can we teach our children to be careful enough to be safe in a frightening world yet loving and outgoing enough to accept their fellow human beings?

Share with your children acceptable ways to interact with others. God lives within each of us, so we can feel and express love for our fellow; God is love, so we are able to be loving. Granted, there are times when it is difficult to love some people. We need to talk about that with our children as well, emphasizing that even the most annoying, demanding people are worthy of love. When you come back into your house after a blow-up with your neighbor over his son's drum practice in the garage at 6 A.M., it's important that your own children realize that your momentary frustration and verbal exasperation does not mean your neighbor is an unworthy person; it is his actions, not the person, that have you so upset. When you have calmed down, explain this to your children. If you've spoken of love before, your children will know that you are frustrated and just blowing off steam—something you can reinforce when you are calmer.

Teach your children to deal with adversaries in a compassionate way. God says to "love your enemies, do good to them which hate you, bless them that curse you" (Luke 6:27–28, KJV) because you will be showing the love of God through yourself. We know that God teaches us to "love thy neighbor as thyself," something extremely difficult for even adults to do when others are annoying. Imagine how much more difficult it is for children to try to love, or at least accept and like, a classmate who ignores them, calls them names, or bullies them. Yet we need to teach children that they are strong enough to meet the challenge of these problems and caring and compassionate enough to deal with the offender, as Kyle did.

Sixteen-year-old Kyle was putting his books into his locker when a fellow student mocked in a voice loud enough for the entire hallway of students to hear, "Hey, jock head, finding your books for class? That's kind of a major cerebral challenge for someone who just got an F on his English test, isn't it?"

Kyle's healthy self-esteem allowed him to show compassion toward his tormentor. "Hey, good morning to you too, Larry. How's it going?" Kyle realized he would feel better about himself by a positive response. And because he did, he felt he had accomplished a real victory in responding from a base of compassion ratter than disrespect.

* * *

Tina's seven-year-old daughter Delia climbed into the car one day after school and huffed, "I hate Susie!" While Tina was a little taken back by her daughter's vehemence, she bit her tongue to keep from jumping in with a denial or scolding and let her go on. "She stuck her tongue out at me and told Roseanna I was stupid—just because I didn't want to play on the dumb monkey bars with her at recess."

Calm, but taking Delia's feelings seriously, Tina said, "Hmm. This isn't the first time you've fought with

Susie, is it?"

"No," Delia answered, "she's always being mean to me."

"Why do you think Susie does this to you?"

Delia gave a typical first response: "Because Susie's mean!"

"Maybe we should understand what things happen before Susie is mean," countered Tina. "Is Roseanna always there when Susie is mean to you?"

"Yes," Delia said.

"Roseanna is your best friend, isn't she?" Another yes from Delia. "Didn't you tell me Susie lives next door to Roseanna?" Affirmative again. "What do you think, are we on to something?" Tina asked. Another nod. "When Susie is only mean when Roseanna is around and wanting to play with you, what do you think makes her be mean?"

"Do you think it's all Roseanna's fault?" Delia asked indignantly.

"No, I don't think it's Roseanna's fault."

After a moment's suspicious inspection, Delia accepted her mother's sincerity. "Well, if it's not Roseanna's fault, why do you think it only happens when she's with Susie and me?"

"Do Susie and Roseanna play a lot together—especially at home?"

"Yeah, cause she's the only one Roseanna has to play with lots of times."

"Well, when you're at school does Roseanna play with her?"

Delia shrugged. "Sometimes, but mostly she plays with me."

"How do you think that makes Susie feel?"

Another shrug, very casual, but Tina could see her point was getting across. "Probably jealous," she answered, a bit disdainfully.

"Probably," Tina agreed. "What does Susie feel like when she feels jealous?"

"I don't know, because I don't get jealous," Delia insisted.

"You don't?"

"When was I jealous?" Delia demanded.

"Well, let me think. What about the time your grandmother took your cousin Eric to the zoo?"

"But that wasn't fair!" Delia protested.

"Well, maybe that's what Susie feels: It isn't fair that Roseanna only plays with her when no one else is available. But I have another question: What else did you feel when you thought your grandmother wasn't being fair to you?"

Tina could see the little wheels in her daughter's head turning. Finally, Delia answered, "I guess I felt mad. But I felt kind of sad, too."

Tina nodded. "So, besides being mad, would you say that part of being jealous is having your feelings hurt?"

"Yeah. . . . Is that how Susie feels?" Tina nodded. "But I'm not the one that will only play with her when no one else is around!"

"Well, let's try and remember—how did you feel and act when Eric told you about his day at the zoo with Grandmom?"

"That's not the same! He was bragging!"

"Come on, he always tells you about special things he does, and it never bothered you before. Was he really bragging, or were you just jealous?"

Delia looked sheepish. "I guess he wasn't bragging. I was mean to him, wasn't I?"

"I'm afraid so. But even though you felt and acted mad, the real reason was something else, wasn't it? What we decided before—about being jealous. So, the reason Susie sometimes acts so mean to you is because . . . ?"

"Her feelings are hurt," Delia supplied. "And that feels bad."

"Let's decide what you should do about Susie being jealous and hurt, OK?"

"Mom, what do *you* think I should do?"

Tina chuckled. "You're taking the easy way. But I think I would try to find ways to make Susie feel less like I was the reason for any unhappiness she felt. How could you do that?"

"Well, I guess I could play with her—ask her if she wanted to play, instead of her just following us around."

"And . . . ?"

"I could be nice, even when she's mean."

"That sounds great, because it sounds loving. Besides

Susie, who would that make happy?"

"It'd make God happy." She smiled. "And that would make me happy!"

This dialogue between mother and daughter shows how children can be helped to realize that they have a huge capacity for loving within themselves. No matter what your children's ages, they need to understand that by giving that love through service to others, they are making themselves and God happier and also enriching their lives.

Show love for others. Aside from teaching your children this principle in words alone, teach by having compassion for the sick, unlovely, and needy. Your actions demonstrate your faith in God. Do your children see you doing good works that are expressions of your love for others? For example, giving to Goodwill? volunteering at school? donating blood? taking time to help a friend who needs it, even when it means some degree of sacrifice? It also may require giving of yourself when you may not want to extend yourself, as Heather found out.

Mr. Fontonelli's daughter Heather picked up the telephone and yelled for her father. "Dad! It's Mr. O'Riley again!" When her father came, she covered the phone and said, "He wants you to come over and work on his car . . . again! Isn't he ever going to leave you alone?

Mr. Fontonelli took the phone and assured his neighbor he would stop over. Then he put his arm around Heather. "Honey, since Mrs. O'Riley passed away, Mr. O'Riley is lonely. He doesn't know what to do with his evenings. He's not ready to accept his wife's death yet, not ready to talk things out. He just needs companionship and to feel that someone cares. Remember how we talked about showing your love for friends in deeds? Mr. O'Riley needs me now. Sure, it's inconvenient, but I'll help him see this through. Your mother understands. She did the same thing when her friend Pamela got a divorce, remember?"

Mr. Fontonelli taught his daughter a lesson she remembers well. "I saw Dad taking the time to do what he had always told us to do."

Five: Your Actions Should Reflect Your Faith

Stephen Covey, in his beautifully written and important book, *The Seven Habits of Highly Effective People,* says that we can't talk ourselves out of something we've behaved our way into. This is bound closely to the universal truth that it isn't words but action that counts.

A church committee of eight met to decide how best to raise the money needed to repair a leak in their church ceiling. Whom should they ask for donations? After about two hours of deliberation and a recommendation to ask the congregation for yet another pledge, one member said, "Look at us. Each of us has resources and yet we are asking others for this sum. Let's raise the needed money, right here and now."

A call to action is supported in many faiths (Moses, *Oneness,* pp. 44–49).

Christianity teaches, "God will render to every man according to his deeds."
Judaism teaches, "Doing is the chief thing."
Taoism teaches, "Not in words does God give answers."
Buddhism teaches, "Like a beautiful flower, full of color, but without scent, are the finest but fruitless words of him who does not act accordingly."

How Do You Teach Your Children to Live Their Faith?

You can't teach what you yourself have not learned. A leader must have walked the path to be a trusted guide. We teach our children to act on the love of God and their faith in several ways.

Live your faith. Your actions will teach your children about acting on their faith. You must live out your words in actions for them to be accepted and respected. If you yourself are not loving and showing your love toward others, it does little good to tell your children to act on their own love. Hearing you say, "Doing something nice or good for someone else is not only helping and giving, it is also living out your faith in God," has far more lasting results if your children see you showing your faith by your own loving actions.

Help children act in a giving manner. Teach your children how these principles can come alive. Even small actions, like taking a sick friend her homework, helping a neighbor carry her groceries from the car to the house, or teaching a small child to tie her shoelaces, can be an act of faith and love. Jesus said that "even a cup of cold water" given in his name is loving God (Matt. 10:42).

For older children, you may want to plan more structured, ambitious ways of giving. For example, there are many charitable organizations that need help in feeding the homeless or putting together fund raisers. A friend of my daughter adopted a foreign child as her means of giving love. You know your children best, what they are interested in, what they are capable of. Include your children in the planning. Allow them to show their own ways of loving and giving. Let the Spirit of God work through your children, and encourage your children to ask God to show them things that would please God to have them do for someone.

Make it a family affair. Find a community service or charitable activity that you can become involved with as a family, or do something that can be done within your home. While some families feel equipped to take in foster children, many of us would be better suited to a family project that involved a simpler activity, such as collecting toys, clothes, and food for those in need. Social responsibility is more complex than goodness. It's more than passing out soup in a soup kitchen for the homeless; it may also mean working legislatively or in other ways to ensure that all people have safe housing and food.

Teach that giving is about personal sharing. Help children feel that giving is a responsibility and a source of satisfaction. While very small children often have strong territorial feelings about their toys, young people of all ages may have difficulty letting go of items that seem a part of them. Even teenagers may not want to give away board games they haven't played in five years. Our children also need to learn they can give of themselves as well—by sharing time with the sick and elderly, by preparing meals for those incapable of doing so themselves, by babysitting for a young mother. There's always time in life to help others. Such acts help your children feel they are helping God to make a better world for all people. In return they experience spiritual growth and joy. There's a bonus in it for us as parents as well: We learn what is important to our children and are better able to relate to their interests and needs, and we see them begin to understand more fully the Christian adage, "You can give without loving, but you can't love without giving."

Here are some simple things you can teach children of all ages to share:

- Toys, games, cassettes, videos, CDs
- A parent's time and attention
- Their feelings about God
- Other things you know they value, such as clothing or bicycles or cars
- Their decisions on what to play or how to spend time
- Health and grooming tips
- Their hugs and kisses (especially with older family members)
- Stories about their day and how school went

Teach social responsibility. Teach your children that God demands that we be socially responsible, that justice is more than kindness or charity. God requires love from us for others. To help your children become involved, you might call a volunteer information center to learn what charitable or social-change organizations have action campaigns or programs that are geared specifically to children, such as UNICEF on Halloween. Have your children participate in a clean-up day, often sponsored by neighborhoods. If there is no clean-up day, involve your children in planning one. Take your children to visit the hospital or the nursing home. Convalescent homes for the elderly often have programs in which younger children play with older people, bringing laughter into their days. Older children might enjoy an "information campaign," in which they research a problem and suggest solutions to it. Friends of mine had their teenage children research the possibility of toxic spills by a railroad that often carried hazardous waste through their neighborhood. The children identified the problem, realized the potential for disaster involved, and set out formulating alternate routes. They spoke to neighborhood groups and to their local council person and raised community awareness about the problem. Groups like Habitat for Humanity work with disadvantaged people to build homes.

Six: Tithing Is Essential

Tithing is one form of learning to act on our love, to give to God's work and to others. Spoken of in the Bible, tithing means giving 10 percent of your income to God. Some people believe this means donating it to a church, while others tithe by giving money to a charity or directly to a needy person. God doesn't *need* our tithes, God wants our hearts. God wants a happy giver, so it is necessary for parents to teach children to give from a loving heart.

How Do You Teach Your Child to Tithe?

Spiritual tithing, according to Webster's dictionary, is giving to support clergy and churches. We are more willing to support a cause we truly believe in than just donate to a charitable organization. Like most parents, you are probably thinking right now, "It took me forever to teach my children just to share their toys, and forever and a day to give a little volunteer time at the shelter. How am I ever going to convince them to give money away, money they would like to use to buy toys or clothes or cassettes?"

Sometimes it seems simple to give away old toys and clothes that we aren't using anyway. Sometimes it doesn't seem like a lot to spend two or three hours on a Thursday afternoon working at a shelter, especially if friends are working there as well. But giving away actual money can be very difficult to do, especially when it seems there isn't enough to go around for our own needs. Have we taught by our own attitude to love and cherish money? God says where our treasure is, there is our heart. Money has its place, but it must not be our God. What is most essential is that we teach that tithing carries on God's work.

Begin when the children are young. When my daughter, Jennifer, was just four years old, I gave her three piggy banks, one pink, one blue, and one clear. Whenever Jennifer received any money, such as for her birthday or Christmas, or earned some cash by helping me with chores around the house, she would divide it among the banks. We agreed that each bank had a purpose. The pink piggy was for tithing. She would use the money in that bank to help others. The blue piggy was for saving. That money would go into her bank account and be left alone for now. The clear piggy was money she could spend any way she wanted (and Jennifer loved the fact that in the clear piggy she could see her money adding up quickly).

Jennifer enjoyed dropping the coins through the slots of the piggy banks and lifting and shaking the banks to try to guess how much money was in them. Each time Jennifer made a deposit, we would go through the ritual together, saying in unison: "Some money for tithing to help others, some money for savings to help me later, and some money for anything I want!" Jennifer came to accept this three part split as normal banking practice.

When the banks became full, we would put the money to its uses together. We'd make a special trip to deposit her savings money in the bank, where I would explain to Jennifer how bankbooks work. The money in the clear piggy bank came along on the trip. We would stop off at the mall on the way home and buy something Jennifer wanted "just because." These were her gifts to herself, something she could buy with her own money. We always greatly enjoyed these mother-daughter outings.

But Jennifer most enjoyed the money from the pink piggy bank. When that bank was full, my daughter and I would sit down and discuss what we should do with it. She herself was allowed to drop it in the collection tray at church. As Jennifer got older, she became more and more involved in deciding which charitable organization should receive contributions, although most of the money still went to the church. A love of animals helped her to decide to donate to a local organization that trains dogs to help the blind.

Tithing is to advance the work of God on earth, and people seem to find varied ways to do so.

Have an organized system. Your children will resent tithing if you spring it on them suddenly. It is important that you have a special system that makes tithing natural and sincere. Although it's good to teach such a system when children are young, it's never too late to start. You can make it easier by reminding them to put some money aside for tithing so they will acquire the habit. The key is to be consistent. It may take a lot of reminding to begin with, but if you continue to mention tithing, and if tithing is taught properly, you engender the feeling that the gift is going to God, as we entrust it to trustworthy people to put it to use as God directs them.

Talk about the tithing's usefulness. We all want to feel that our contributions are doing something worthwhile. Even if your children feel their incomes are so small that the tiny bit they tithe is almost inconsequential, show them it can make a difference. Talk about how their contribution might be going to improved nutrition for a poor child, who then is able to study and concentrate better and possibly become a physician with a cure for cancer. Think about how those few dollars allowed great things to be done because your child cared enough to give, so God's kindness to other people would be shown through you and your sharing in God's great and mighty work on earth.

10

*Five More Universal Truths
to Teach Your Children*

Your children must believe they are loved by God, assured that God is caring for them, watching over them, loving and accepting them unconditionally. When children believe they are loved by God, others can love them too. They come to love themselves as they feel a sense of worth and value. As their faith grows, children become aware of their talents and blessings. Children then can emerge with the confidence and assurance that their lives have purpose. Knowing God's love plays a vital role in keeping the joy and peace and fruits of the Spirit alive within your children.

Seven: Our Inner Self Directs Our Life

A friend told me about her brother, who thought of himself as unworthy. He possessed woefully little self-esteem. As early as his adolescent years, he frequently had episodes of depression. Soon he began to consider himself a depressed person. His depression defined who he was. The cycle was simple. What Robert originally thought of himself created certain feelings. Those feelings became part of who he was and caused him to act in accordance with those feelings. He then became the way he acted: depressed. Of course, there are many physical causes of depression that require medical treatment. However, there are countless examples of people who have been cured of depression (and even of physical trauma) through the power of their faith, through their acceptance of God as a part of their lives. The principle involved is simple but eloquent: When your children accept God into their hearts and feel loved and accepted, they become loving and accepting toward others.

How Do You Teach Your Children That Their Inner Selves Direct Their Lives?

Encourage your children to think positive thoughts. It sounds simplistic, but it works. This holds true for children of all ages. Even the seemingly jaded teenager needs to be told to concentrate on the positive things in life, to think about "whatever is true, whatever is honorable, whatever is just, whatever is pure, whatever is lovely" (Phil. 4:8). Encourage your children to practice spiritual positive thinking. Discuss situations in which a positive spiritual attitude can make all the difference. Draw examples from the children's own lives. If your children are old enough, recommend good books or inspired music. The Suggested Reading section in the back of this book provides resources, and you may wish to ask your public librarian or chaplain, spiritual leader, or spiritual soulmate for additional suggestions.

Tell your children repeatedly how special and loved they are. Discuss the importance of being loved by God, of being filled with God's love. Show examples of the strength that knowledge of God's love can give. If your earthly father loves you and gives you good things, how much more will God give? (See Luke 11:13).

Remind your children that God loves others too and expects us to treat others with love. Much of children's self-concept is wrapped up in how others see and treat them. If the kids at school think your daughter is a brain, she will see herself that way. If, unfortunately, they think she is dull, she will see herself that way. It's important for children to feel accepted and admired by their peers. Discuss with your children how they feel when others praise or criticize them, then lead them to see how others feel when we criticize or praise their actions. Remind them that God loves us all, and wants us to love one another. We are reminded to "take the log out of your own eye and then you will see to take the speck out of your brother's eye" (Matt. 7:5). Criticism and praise have their own fruit.

Twelve-year-old Lena wanted to invite all her classmates to her birthday party except for one—Nancee. When her mother told her she had to invite all the girls, that it would be unfair to exclude anyone, Lena countered with "But Mom, she walks funny and dresses weird. No one really likes her."

"Lena," said her mother, "God loves her as much as you. Don't you think you would feel better about yourself if you shared some of that love, if you showed Nancee you accept and admire her too? God's love is not limited because of peculiarities and handicaps. Surely there is something about her that you can compliment."

"The other kids will think I'm weird if I hang around with this girl," complained Lena.

"God wants what's best for you and her and will give you the strength to be friendly," reassured her mother.

As Lena told her mother after the party, "She was so happy to be invited, Mom. And I think all the girls like her now."

Teach your children that being friendly, sensitive, and showing mercy is god like. We are not God, but we can be god like. Spiritual teaching adds to our children's spiritual safety. Unless children have this inner security, they will not have the power to stand up to the temptation to make the destructive or less virtuous choice. Our children need to have a belief in God's presence with them, and God's love and acceptance of them, in order to live confidently and peacefully.

Rejoice that God wants what's best for us all. Children sometimes equate God with rules and regulations, with things that should *not* be done. It's important to show them that God wants them to be happy, that God wants children to believe they have talents and gifts and can use these gifts for good for themselves, as well as for others. Many passages in the Bible encourage people to "rejoice in the Lord always." Jesus taught that he had come in order that we "might have life, and have it more abundantly." Teaching your children to believe these things can help them think about the things that are part of their spiritual safety, encouraging the growth of self-confidence and joy in life.

Eight: Be Still and Know . . .

The Bible and other sacred scriptures encourage us to "Be still, and know that I am God" (Ps. 46:10). In addition to the truths, precepts, and prayers we teach our children, we must encourage them to be still and think of God.

Children lead such active lives they need to understand the benefits of contemplation and meditation, and a quietness of soul where God communes with them. "Draw near to God and he will draw near to you" (James 4:8). When I was a young child I learned a beautiful song that, when I would sing or hum it, put me in tune with that quiet place inside. It is called "In the Garden" (words and music by C. Austin Miles), and it goes this way:

> I come to the garden alone,
> While the dew is still on the roses,
> And the voice I hear
> Falling on my ear,
> The Son of God discloses.
>
> And he walks with me and he talks with me,
> And he tells me I am his own,
> And the joy we share as we tarry there,
> None other has ever known.
>
> He speaks and the sound of his voice
> Is so sweet the birds hush their singing,
> And the melody that he gave to me
> Within my heart is ringing.
>
> And he walks with me and he talks with me,
> And he tells me I am his own,
> And the joy we share as we tarry there,
> None other has ever known.

How Do You Help Your Children to Be Still?

Make time for their communion with God. The day can slip away so quickly, with soccer practice, homework, chores, chatting on the telephone, and the hundred and one other things that children feel they have to do. Set aside about five minutes daily. Schedule this time just as you would schedule dinner or sports practice, and don't allow a cancellation. When we are calm we think more lucidly and are more apt to be receptive to the precious truths that are within. God meets our deepest needs and yearnings best at times when we are quiet and focused on our spiritual thirsts.

Don't let quiet time be something children do only when there's nothing else to do. Quiet time can be worked into the schedule according to your children's ages. For example, if your children are preschoolers, you might make prayer time and quiet time right before their naps. If they are teenagers, you could encourage them to slow down just before dinner.

Talk about communing with God. Children have days when they are nervous, anxious, rambunctious. They might already know they are too stressed out and be looking for something to help them calm down. Speak with them about turning to God for help. While exercise, relaxation techniques, and the like are great stress reducers, a few minutes of thinking, meditating, and praying can help refresh children and calm them down at the same time. They can get in touch with what is bothering them and ask for guidance and help in dealing with it. During quiet times, the voice of God that is within all of us can be heard more clearly.

Use quiet time to be thankful for God's good things. The busier we are, the more we seem to complain about problems and difficulties of life. When we sit still and think, we have a chance to realize how blessed we truly are. We have a few moments to be thankful for all our gifts: God, health, family, friends. Spiritual communion provides children with a time for wonderment to slow down and see what their lives are truly about.

Nine: Children Need Spiritual Wisdom

"From childhood you have been acquainted with the sacred writings which are able to instruct you for salvation" (2 Tim. 3:15). The teachings of most faiths support the belief that children are never too young to absorb spiritual ideologies (Moses, *Oneness*, pp. 88–89).

> *Judaism teaches: "My son, gather instruction from thy youth up; so shalt thou find wisdom till thine old age."*
> *Hinduism teaches: "Knowledge is riches, what one learns in youth is engraven on stone."*
> *Islam teaches: "Seek knowledge from the cradle to the grave."*
> *Buddhism teaches: "He who, even as a young student, applies himself to the doctrine of truth brightens up this world like the moon set free from the clouds."*

How Do You Teach Your Children to Seek Spiritual Wisdom?

Older children are very often afraid of being alienated from their friends if they practice or act on their spiritual beliefs. Unfortunately, more and more children today have had little if any exposure to spiritual teachings. Let your children know that you consider teaching spirituality as much of a parental responsibility as teaching them to tie their shoes, ride a bicycle, and drive a car.

Identify the values you cherish and want to instill. Actions are based on beliefs, which in turn are based on values. Your values are the first step; everything you believe and do comes from them. It is therefore critical that you try to be clear in your own mind which values you most cherish. Some of them are universal: kindness, forgiveness, charity. Others may be more or less important to you depending on your culture and background. In order for your children to begin understanding their role in this life, you must first make clear to them what is important, what will be the underlying foundation of their lives. We are to love God, ourselves, and our fellow human beings, in that order. This is a good beginning in identifying priorities for spiritual safety.

Teach the principles, including right and wrong, that can guide actions. You want to show your children how actions have consequences, and that children themselves must eventually assume responsibility for their actions. Again, there are certain principles that most of us cherish—as given in the Ten Commandments—and others that will be important to you personally. Part of responsible parenting is helping children distinguish right from wrong. Simply telling children, "Don't do this, don't do that" is not effective. You must build a bridge of understanding that helps children understand *why* they should or shouldn't do or believe something. As the adage says, "As the sapling is bent, so it grows."

Define the spiritual building blocks that lead to wisdom. Adults toss around words like love, joy, peace, self-control, kindness, goodness, and patience and assume that children know what these terms mean. They may have only a fuzzy understanding of what we mean or may have a completely different understanding from what we hope they have. For example, take self-control and patience.

Children are taught that self-control is necessary, but they rarely understand what the expression means. The following examples, for various age groups, may help you explain the idea to your children.

- Self-control is listening to your friend's problems without jumping in and talking about yours, or hearing about your friend's successes without showing any envy. Spiritual self-control means listening to your heart. We are reminded to "rejoice with those who rejoice and weep with those who weep" (Rom. 12:15).

- Self-control can mean waiting until after dinner to have your dessert or skipping candy altogether to lose weight or prevent cavities. The controlling of our personal appetites, whatever they may be, can lead us to a greater dependence on God for strength to succeed.

- Sometimes self-control means not laughing at someone who does something embarrassing, like tripping or giving a dumb answer in class. Self-control is also shown when you don't jump in and give the right answer to show up someone else.

- It takes self-control not to push your little sister when she has just hit you or made you very angry.

- Self-control means being quiet in the classroom when you are bursting with news to tell your best friend. It means sitting quietly and rechecking your answers when you have finished an exam, rather than just getting up and leaving.

You may summarize the concept of self-control by telling your children that it is thinking and deciding what the right thing to do is, then doing what you decided is right.

Patience can also be explained to children using everyday examples. Patience has been said to be the most virtuous when we can let the sick and slow of mind and limb stop us in our busy lives, and we assist in gentleness and sincerity the less gifted.

- Patience means waiting for your brother to wake up from his nap instead of waking him up yourself because you want to play with him.
- Patience means standing in line and waiting your turn when the ice cream truck stops on your street.
- Patience is quietly waiting for your parents to finish their dinner at a restaurant, even if they linger over their coffee and you are eager to get home to watch a TV show or listen to a new cassette.
- Patience can be waiting for your turn to use the crayon your friend is coloring with or waiting for your sibling to get off the telephone.
- Patience is the setting aside of self for a short while in submission to another's needs, demands, or wants and doing so in a loving manner.

Ten: Ask and You Will Be Answered

In Luke 18:1–8 and 1 Thessalonians 5:17, Jesus encourages his disciples to be persistent in their prayers and tells a parable that illustrates the kind of persistence and patience that may be required in seeing that our prayers are answered. "Ask, and it will be given you; seek, and you will find; knock and [the door] will be opened to you" (Matt. 7:7). These are encouraging promises for parents to share with their children.

How Do You Teach Your Children That to Ask Brings Answers?

Parenting would be so much easier if we could simply tell our children something and have them immediately accept it as true and act upon it. But the questioning starts during the two's and continues through the teenage years. We need more than just words to help our children believe that prayers will be answered. People of all faiths believe and testify to God's answering. Begin by relating your own experiences of answered prayers.

Demonstrate your belief in prayer. You yourself must believe that when you ask God for something, your prayers are heard and answered. Let your children know that you pray for help and guidance and tell them of the results of the prayers. Saying "I asked God to give me guidance on what direction I should take in making this decision" shows your child the day-to-day relationship you have with God through prayer. We are listened to by an all-knowing God who loves us.

Teach that God answers prayers. Children (as well as many adults) believe that "ask and you shall receive" means they have carte blanche to get whatever they want. Children especially can come to view God as a sort of Santa Claus; just make a list and sit back and expect the goodies to come in. How many times have you seen your own children praying for a new bike, a skateboard, a laser disc system? It's important to teach children that God answers prayers of all sorts, not just ones demanding material possessions. God gives us what we need, and more, *as our sovereign,* not our get-it-for-us God. We need to respect God.

Talk to your children about the value of prayers in obtaining strength to do the right thing, such as studying for an exam, instead of praying to get an A. The cliché "God helps those who help themselves" is valid. Children need to know that God is there to provide the intangibles, such as patience, self-control, strength of character, and wisdom, not just the more tangible things.

Prepare children to accept God's answers. Children confidently expect that when they pray to God, they will get what they want. It's important to know that, when they ask, they will be given an answer . . . but it is God's answer, not necessarily their own. God knows what is best for us and will answer our prayers accordingly. We may not get the answer we were expecting, but we have to live with the belief that the answer we get is what will help us most in the long run. It is very difficult for children to understand and accept the "this is for your own good; you'll be grateful later" idea when something they prayed for doesn't come through. You as a parent need to prepare your children to seek God's answer, whatever it may be. When your children question seemingly unanswered prayers, teach them to rely on the help of their church community in learning more about God's will. Bible study also guides us to understand God's will in new ways.

Teach children patience in waiting for God's answer. In this high-speed world, children are accustomed to instant gratification. They want an answer, and they want it now. We parents try to instill patience in children, telling them, "Yes, we will discuss that subject, but not right now." That same patience must be present in waiting for an answer from God. Children need to understand that praying is not like ordering from a catalog; there is no guaranteed delivery date. Show that your faith is constant, that you know you will get an answer.

We must have trust and believe that God's timing is best. God's delays are not denials. Your Spirit-prompted prayers will be answered. Don't let the waiting time weaken your faith. You might think about the following questions and then ask your children the same ones: "What requests have you been waiting for God to answer? What have you been learning while waiting? Has your faith grown or weakened as a result? What circumstances make it hard to wait on God? How do we know that if we wait on God we won't be disappointed?"

Eleven: You Reap What You Sow

This vibrant, meaningful expression has become a cliché, so we tend to forget just what it really means. There is a wonderful promise contained within. Religions around the world have accepted the wisdom of this saying for thousands of years. (Moses, *Oneness*, pp. 40–41).

> *Buddhism teaches: "It is nature's rule that as we sow we shall reap."*
> *Christianity teaches: "Whatever a man sows, that he will also reap."*
> *Hinduism teaches: "Thou canst not gather what thou dost not sow; as thou dost plant the tree so will it grow."*
> *Sikhism teaches: "Whatever man soweth, that shall he reap."*

How Do You Teach Your Children That They Reap What They Sow?

If you plant grapes, you get grapes; thistles, you get this-tles. "Train up a child in the way he should go, and when he is old he will not depart from it" (Prov. 22:6). "Sow the wind, and . . . reap the whirlwind" (Hos. 8:7).

"Billy hit me!"

"Well, you deserved it; you pinched me!"

How rich you would be if you had a dollar for every time you heard those lines! All parents are used to chil-dren passing blame for their actions to others. "I didn't mean to be late; Cynthia made me!" Part of growing up is accepting responsibility for one's own actions. We can phrase this another way in teaching spirituality: You reap what you sow. You get what you give. What goes around comes around. The fact that there are so many clichés on this topic shows that people have recognized its importance for a long time. Children need to understand the connection between their deeds and the consequences. We have been taught to believe that our thoughts can bring about reality; even intentions can lead to consequences.

Create spiritual safety by protecting innocence. Children are born innocent of worldly prejudices and experiences, but their natures have an inherent tendency to be self-focused and demanding. Temperaments expose themselves almost at birth. The tone of a baby's first cries can tell us something about its inborn disposition. Children are not born feeling bigotry or hatred, destructiveness or overweening ambition. Yet they are imposed on every day and learn these negatives. Television, for example, teaches all sorts of stereotyping and violent ideas. If we sow these poison seeds in the young minds of our children, is it surprising that they harvest such people?

We must teach and guide our children to be sharing, caring, and loving. The beauty of it is that children are trusting and eager learners. Unfortunately, they learn bad with the same openness. If we want to reap ambrosia, we must use the right recipe and take pains to keep our children spiritually safe. We can do this by awareness, persistence, and constant precautions.

- Be aware of the company your children keep and the clubs and organizations they join. We become like the things we admire.

- Know what books and magazines your children read. As the mind is fed, it is nourished and then produces its harvests. The mind is too precious to trash with junk materials.
- Take time to learn about television shows and movies, to determine which ones are and are not appropriate viewing for your children. Our eyes help indoctrinate our minds and this influences our behavior, and we are either inspired or scarred.
- Set your standards, make certain your children are aware of them and understand them, and then enforce them. Teach your children that they are accountable to God for the use of their lives; and responsible to their family and country.

Provide examples from your own life. As with most things, you show by example and by discussion. When you take the time to say to your children, "I'm so happy with the relationship I have with your teacher; I know it was worth going even though I had to leave work to do so," you allow your children to see the connection between the action and the reaction. When your son does well on his spelling test, remind him that his hard work and hours of study and memorization paid off. If your daughter doesn't pass a physics exam, ask whether the time she spent at the movies might have been better spent studying. It's important to show the connection between effort put in and results achieved.

Be consistent in your guidance and discipline. Guidance and discipline are the epitome of the "As ye sow, so shall ye reap" principle. Good discipline is never cruel but, rather, corrective. When you explain the behavior you expect from your children and they do otherwise, they need to reap the appropriate consequences. If you let your children get away with something once and then lower the boom on them the next time, you are not making the connection between activity and response. Discipline and punishment are not the same. Discipline is an act of love to guide and teach. Punishment is about fair and consistent consequences.

Discuss the bigger picture. Make it clear to your children that specific actions come back to us in the general way we live our lives. When we are kind and giving, we can rejoice in it. When we are mean-spirited, petty, and selfish, we are deprived of many joys.

Do You Need Answers for Yourself?

If you did not grow up in a particularly religious or spiritual environment yourself, you may be feeling lost and alone right now, without an idea of where to begin. Perhaps you need more information yourself. Maybe you know the ideas you want to get across but have lost touch in communicating with your children effectively, or perhaps you're having difficulty getting them to understand the concepts you're trying to explain. You can make learning about spirituality fun and interesting. The following tools may help. They can build spiritual security, wisdom, and acceptance of vital precepts of conduct and values in children.

Spiritual songs. Hymns are wonderful tools. They teach truth and the knowledge of God and provide a wonderful nurturing, sharing experience when you hold your child close and sing them. You can begin singing songs to your children even before their birth and continue forever. With older children, you can sing the words together and think about their meanings. These songs can impart wonderful feelings of love, peace, and joy.

Almost all children love singing. You probably can remember times from your own past when you had sing-alongs or were walking down the street humming your favorite song, oblivious of the passersby. If you can share songs from your own past with your children, wonderful. If you can't think of any songs, you might try finding tapes at the library or at an inspirational bookstore. Videos of such songs, with children singing or with animated characters acting out the lyrics, can be a lot of fun.

Spiritual stories. Spiritual stories can provide your children with understanding and direction. There are picture books for very young children that are easy to understand and gently teach spiritual principles. Biographies often teach of godly people who have succeeded despite obstacles or self-doubts. Reading to your children is always special; these spiritual stories add a new dimension to your relationship to each other and to God.

If you are in a situation where the company your children keep is not very spiritual and their friends are perhaps not the best examples, books can provide good role models. Older children might enjoy reading about spiritually enlightened people such as Mother Teresa or Gandhi. Religious bookstores usually have a section for small children and for teenagers.

Church or fellowship groups. Perhaps due to bad experiences in their own childhoods or because they are just uncomfortable with the idea of dogma or judgments, some parents may feel there are no churches in which they would feel comfortable. They pay lip service to the idea of finding God all around them, and avoid the many benefits that organized worship can provide.

Churches offer the sort of strength epitomized in the "in numbers there is strength" principle. Jesus said that where two or more were gathered in his name, he would be there. God lives within each of us; we each have our own idea of God and God's teachings. This means that we each have something unique to share with others, making church an enlightening and eye-opening experience. We are encouraged and strengthened in our faith by being around others of like mind. This is especially important for children, who have a strong need to fit in. Going to church can give children a feeling of community and oneness with others. It provides structure to the family's act of giving and love, providing new opportunities for closeness.

A final point: As children grow, they tend to discount much of what their parents tell them and look to outside sources for new information verifying old information (you parents of teenagers know this very well!). But when your children are attending church regularly, they will find friends and teachers and others who are likely to counsel them based on the spiritual teachings and lessons you want your children to learn.

Prayer. When Paul wrote the Ephesians about how to protect themselves spiritually, he encouraged them to "Pray at all times in the Spirit " (Eph. 6:18). If you mention spiritual beliefs and subjects and pray only by rote at mealtime grace or before bedtime, you haven't shown your children the true richness of prayer. You want to make prayer a regular part of your everyday existence, but not something memorized and muttered at certain times. Children live what they see. Children who grow up seeing their parents believing in God's existence and ability to hear and answer their prayers learn to believe in the power of prayer at a young age and will remember what they have seen and heard, even if they seem to reject their faith later. It will be with them for the rest of their lives.

Communication. Often during adolescence, children turn their backs on those spiritual principles and values their parents have taught them. For most parents, especially those who have diligently worked on instilling these values, this can be a very painful time. Although the rebellion shouldn't be taken too lightly, remember that the children may not be stating what they believe in their heart of hearts, but only displaying their independence. Once the youngsters feel more comfortable with their identities, they generally return to the beliefs that were so much a part of their growth and life.

Communication is the key. Recall your own feelings at that age and be assured that training and love usually win out in the end.

We have the awesome responsibility of parenting and need to accept the source of comfort we find in knowing we are being guided and assisted by a God who loves parents and children alike. We are the transmission center for the generation ahead. We hold a baton, so to speak, to be passed on in ethics, values, and faith. We know we cannot and should not always prevent unpleasant situations from happening to our children, and we can take heart that a God of love, mercy, and justice is their God as well as ours. We can find comfort in Romans 5:3–5, where Paul reminds us we can "rejoice in our sufferings, knowing suffering produces endurance, and endurance produces character, and character produces hope, and hope does not disappoint us, because God's love has been poured into our hearts through the Holy Spirit which has been given to us."

Spiritual principles help us to find meaning and provide a living anchor for our lives.

V

Keeping Your Children Safe Intellectually

11

Are You Helping Your Children Become Lifelong Learners?

We parents take great precautions to ensure that our children are physically safe. We provide a secure environment with love and acceptance. We strive to exemplify our faith, instill values, and imbue our children with high ideals. That we help our children to develop their potential, to become all they are capable of becoming, is very important. It's the task of parents to see that their children truly discover their individual aptitude and act on that potential.

We often say the words "I want my children to develop their full potential" but are sometimes reluctant to carry it out. For example, do we fund our school classrooms as though we're serious about wanting the best for our children? I think not. That's another reason why your children's potential is in your hands for safekeeping. Children need someone who is willing to champion them. Once again, parents are the key.

The Desire to Learn Begins at Home

We all want our children to experience school success, to be adequately prepared for holding down a job, and to be able to support themselves and a given lifestyle. School success is just one measure of developing intellectual capacities. How do we help our children to develop their full potential, to live consciously rather than sleepwalk through life, to be responsive to the needs of others, to live life to the fullest? The first step is to help our children become learners for life. Whether or not our children remain curious about themselves and the world around them depends on us, their parents. We influence our children's potential from the time they are born, maybe even at the prenatal stage.

Children Are Curious Beings

When our children are little, it seems as if their need to explore the world around them is endless. They are so busy touching, tasting, listening, and looking that their learning often seems like destruction. Yet all too often that curiosity seems to wither, or worse, fade away. Teachers say "the lights went out"; parents refer to their children as "dull." Yet great scholars—from Plato, Socrates, and Aristotle, to Maria Montessori, to modern scholars such as Jaime Escalante—shake up our notion of potential and show us that all children have an enormous capacity to learn, if we truly wish to teach them. Every child can learn; it's all in the approach.

Parents Are Teachers Too

You needn't have a formal degree to teach. Parents are the greatest teachers in the world. I know parents, and I'm sure you do too, who against all odds have taught a child with special needs to be far more than was thought possible. In this regard I think of Chris Burke, the charismatic and gifted television actor, star of *Life Goes On,* who was born with Down's syndrome. Chris was fortunate enough to have parents who believed in helping him achieve more than what others thought a disabled child was capable of. To appreciate the full significance of Chris's story is to be reminded that, unlike many forms of retardation, Down's syndrome is the result of one too many chromosomes, giving children born with this condition an uncanny similarity in appearance and a ceiling on development and potential—or so it was thought. It is believed that the average life span for an individual with Down's syndrome is twenty-five to thirty years; with an IQ peaking around 75, abilities are severely limited. When Chris was born in 1965, physicians recommended that parents place babies with Down's syndrome in institutions before they became attached to them. The majority of such institutions did virtually nothing more than physical caretaking.

Chris surged beyond these commonly held expectations to create a new reality. How? What made the difference? Chris's parents refused to treat him differently from their three other children. They placed a supreme emphasis on self-reliance and achievement and started sensory stimulation, motor exercises, and language instruction immediately, as they did for their other children. Now in his twenties, Chris Burke proudly displays a framed poster with the words OBSTACLES ARE WHAT YOU SEE WHEN YOU TAKE YOUR EYES OFF THE GOAL. Chris calls these words his blueprint for his goal of aspiring to be a full-time actor. At age twelve Chris ran in the Special Olympics. He proudly announced he had come in third and lined up for hugs and handshakes along with the winner. There were only three runners in the race! You need only meet him for a moment to feel the power of his presence and share in the glee of his unmistakable wit. "I don't think of it as Down's syndrome," he says matter-of-factly. "I call it Up syndrome."

The desire to learn is a gift—a legacy to our children. You can develop your children's desire to learn in several ways.

Instill an appreciation of learning. Show your children that you value learning for the sake of being aware and informed. Talk with admiration about friends or acquaintances who share information and stories of interest based on what they know or have experienced. Help your children develop an interest in knowing more about themselves and others, their world, and its galaxies. Your example teaches joy, curiosity, and love of learning.

Set a good example. Your children will follow in your footsteps. When they see you are an ongoing learner reading newspapers, books, and magazines, they are more likely to read also. In turn, hold family discussions about what you are learning.

Stimulate their curiosity. Aside from starting early to provide your children with stimulation through touching, playing patty-cake and other childhood games designed to stimulate learning (as well as encouraging parent-child bonding), plan family outings that trigger your child's curiosity. If a child is studying Egyptian history, go to the museum and look at the exhibits. If the subject is physics, go to a science museum with hands-on games and displays making theory come alive. To encourage music appreciation, take your children to concerts.

Instill an appreciation of schooling. Talk about the importance of getting an education. If you show your children that education is important to you, it will become important to them as well. When you attend an evening course at a local university or discuss the seminar you recently attended at the company you work for, you set an example of the importance of learning.

Show interest in your children's school work. Showing an active interest in school and homework sends the message that you care about your children's learning, and they should too. You're conveying the message that school is purposeful and learning is important.

Of course our children do spend significant time away from us. A child will spend approximately fifteen thousand hours from kindergarten through twelfth grade in an educational system. From five years of age until eighteen, your children will spend nearly eight hours each day during the week in a school environment or in school-related activities. How is that school experience molding your children? Are you involved, or do you see it as a "school" issue? Are your children learning the lessons you hoped they would learn?

Helping Your Children to Manage Their Workplace

You want your children to have positive, rewarding experiences in school to ensure that they will see the value of education and continue to learn throughout their lives. You want them to feel challenged by school, not overwhelmed by it. You want them to feel safe intellectually, as well as emotionally, secure in the knowledge that hard work will pay off, that they can get the job done. For many children, school is an intensely frustrating experience. But it needn't be. You can help your children develop skills in managing school, their world of work.

Twenty-two Things You Can Do

1. Help your children to get organized. Every child needs the appropriate tools to get working: a quiet study area, safe from interruption, equipped with good light, a desk, and a bookcase. Shop for pencils, paper, and standard supplies. Set up a file. The filing cabinet can be the standard kind, or it can be as simple as a large cardboard box divided with inserts separating files in terms of contents ("great articles: save for reports") or by subject area, or, if your child is a fifth-grader or older, more detailed headings, such as "English exams," "English notes to study for semester exam," "English papers handed back," and so on. What's important is that you help your children learn organization. They are, after all, career students.

Next, get a large month-at-a-glance calendar to record work assignments and school-related activities. This makes it easy for children to see when they need to focus on particular projects and assignments and when they are free for social activities. It also helps them feel like serious students doing a job.

This should be the child's work space and, if possible, not shared. It doesn't have to be a large area, just a space associated with doing homework. Not having a place to work, or the tools to do it, is a big reason why many children don't want to study at home.

2. Set parameters on study time. During study time, there should be no TV or Walkman and no phone calls. Phone calls can be made after homework is done or between studying different subjects as a way to take a break. If a child needs to clarify an assignment by talking to a fellow student, two to three minutes are sufficient. If your children have unrestricted phone privileges, discourage lengthy phone calls during study time. You want to teach the power of uninterrupted concentration. Explain why this is a good practice.

3. Agree on a regular time for studying. Whether you decide that this time is immediately after school or after the evening meal, keep it consistent when possible. This routine helps your children do homework consistently day after day and takes away their excuses for not having time to do it.

4. Help your children to identify their work styles. A child may be able to complete all studying and homework in a single session or may do better by studying for twenty minutes, taking a break, and then going back to work. Each child is different. The important thing is to recognize one's own style and optimum pattern for producing the best work. You can help your children identify their work styles by pointing out the rituals that you yourself go through before you are ready for productive work, such as organizing your desk and sharpening all your pencils, even those you don't use.

If a child is overtired or unwilling to get into a particular assignment, what rituals help prepare for productive work: putting on a good tape, a brisk walk, a ten-minute bike ride? Help children learn how to renew their energy and channel it to the tasks that need to be done. It varies for each child, and you're the best judge of that. When my daughter was in fifth and sixth grades, for example, I would allow her to take her bike to the local mini-market for fifty cents' worth of junk food. She couldn't do too much damage with fifty cents, but she did get a surge of energy (my goal) from riding her bike there. I would time her to see if she could get there and back in fifteen minutes. It worked. By the time she came running excitedly into the house to see if she had won against the timer, her endorphins (body proteins that, through exercise, trigger a natural high) were providing her with renewed energy. She was then ready to do her chores and homework before dinner. When she became a seventh-grader, she would no longer buy that, and I had to look for new ways to get her ready to confront two hours or more of homework.

Look for ways that work with your children. If you know a child is simply too tired, don't force it. No one can be productive who is unable to summon the needed energy.

5. Ask meaningful questions about schoolwork. If you ask, "What did you do in school today?" and your child answers, "Nothing," ask more specific questions based on what you know is being taught. Rather than asking, "How was your day?" to which the reply is, "Fine," ask something specific.

- "Do you feel you are making improvement?"
- "What contributed to the good grades as well as to the poor ones?"
- "What is your favorite subject? Why?"
- "Is the A a mark of achievement, or was the work too easy?"
- "Was the D because you didn't understand the material, or was it because the test came the day after the three-day band trip and you weren't prepared?"

Ask these questions even though you may feel you know the answers. Become familiar with the courses a child is enrolled in and know what's being taught and what's expected. Ask questions of the teachers too.

- "What books will be read?"
- "How much homework will be required?"

- "What major long-term projects can be anticipated?"
- "Is my child likely to need help with any special projects?"

Remember, school is tough for A students too.

Your attitude is all-important. Children do as their parents do, not as they say. If you get excited about new books and new ideas, your children will also. Half an hour a day reading and talking to a child makes a big difference. A brief conversation now and then, showing your children that their education is important to you, will influence how they do in school.

6. Determine what on-the-job skills your children need. Use clues from report cards, teacher conferences, and aptitude tests to become familiar with a child's strengths and weaknesses so you'll know where you can help. Is a particular skill lacking that holds the child back? Can you obtain special tutoring for a problem area? Is there a physical problem, perhaps with eyesight or hearing? Is there a particular learning disability? Solution: emphasize the child's strengths, show understanding of the weaknesses, and help overcome them.

7. Ask about "coworkers." Who are your children's friends at school and why? How much time do they get to be together in favorite school activities? Do they eat lunch together? Who are the good students and why? Who are not such good students and why? Have they noticed that they are better learners when they feel like friends, and better friends when they feel successful in school? What are their thoughts about this realization?

8. Talk to your children about their teachers. Think about the teachers you had in school, the ones you liked and those you didn't. How did they make you want to learn? Were some teachers so exciting that you looked forward to their classes? Did a few teachers even talk with students rather than lecture at them day after day? Did you notice that in some classes time flew by when in others you were often daydreaming, waiting for the class to get over? Do your children like their teachers? Why or why not? What teachers do your children find exciting, and why? In most cases, children choose a career based on a special teacher. Who is this special teacher for each of your children?

9. Teach time-management skills. For most children, whether in elementary, junior high, or high school, there never seems to be enough time outside of school to cope with assignments, friends, extracurricular activities, and family, with personal time left over. Even during the school day, one of the greatest pressures is time. A very important step in helping your youngster learn to manage time is to set up a daily or weekly "to do" list. It should not be long and detailed but should contain those things that he or she wants to accomplish each day or week.

Priority setting is also important. Show how you set priorities, how your management of time allows you to do the things you want to do. Help your child generate the "to do" list and then highlight one or two tasks that are the most urgent. Set a schedule and estimate the length of time necessary to perform each task. Break long-term projects down into manageable parts so the child can begin on them, not wait until the last minute to do something that can't be completed in a short period of time.

10. Help with homework judiciously. When children become students, parents often become students too. This can be a very frustrating and tension-filled experience for both parent and child. Not all parents are able to help their children with homework. If you find that you are unable to help your child, for whatever reason, find an outside source. Children do enjoy working with others, and this can alleviate the tension and additional constraints on parental time. For example, teenagers and college students enjoy working with younger children.

When you are helping your children with homework, here are some things to keep in mind:

- Have patience. Allow for learning at your child's own pace.
- Encourage your child to do good work but recognize that this work may not necessarily be A-level.
- Let your children know that you are proud of them for doing their best.
- Allow time to relax between difficult or long assignments.
- Praise positive efforts as well as work achievements.
- Don't name-call when children are having a rough time grasping a concept.
- Don't *you* get discouraged.

11. Tutor. Aside from daily assignments, there may be an area where a child needs special help in acquiring a skill. Tutoring your own child is often a difficult undertaking. I'm not sure I've met too many parents or children who have enjoyed one another in these roles. Remember, the important thing is enhancing your child's sense of capability, while preserving the relationship between the two of you.

When you're ready to help, this approach works best. "Michael, I talked to your math teacher this morning. She told me you were doing well with simple equations, but that you were having some problems with graphing. I can help you with graphing for a little while. How does that sound to you?" This opens the lines of communication.

Remember that you want him to want the extra help. You want his participation and commitment to do better. Without it, you may be the only one working for improvement. Here are some special considerations when tutoring.

- Sit next to your child rather than across the desk. This way it's easy for both of you to see the lesson, and it encourages a friendlier relationship.

- If you find that the tutoring session is unpleasant for you or your child, don't get discouraged, and don't react. Just listen awhile. Your child's reaction may be based on fear of not being able to do the work, while not wanting you to know it for fear you'll be let down. For example, if you find a child is giving you any answer just so you will be frustrated and go away, you might say, "Let's go more slowly. I'll be patient while you think this through. I have lots of time."

- Be sure the directions you give are presented slowly and clearly. For some children the major difficulty is not in mastering the subject matter but in following directions.

- Work through one step at a time. This keeps your child's attention on the work and gives you a closer look at where the difficulties lie. For example, if you are doing addition problems, present them one at a time rather than asking your child to do a page of fifteen or twenty problems all at once.

- When your child speaks or when you are speaking, be sure to make eye contact. It's sometimes easier to see confusion and frustration than it is to hear it.

- Don't skip any problems. Wait for an answer to each one. This helps your child develop the habit of working on difficult items rather than passing them by.

- Minimize your use of phrases such as "That's wrong." Instead, respond to a wrong answer by restating the question and supplying your child with more clues to help in getting the correct answer. After a correct answer, it's useful to go over the question in its original form, without the clues but with praise.

12. Make homework fun! There is no need to be too serious. It's much more enjoyable to work together when you can gently tease each other or make silly puns. Personalize the lessons with humor. Parents of small children know how much children enjoy it when the parent is wrong: "You mean K-A-T is not how to spell cat?"

13. Follow your child's progress. Performance appraisals or report cards tell how your child is doing overall. However, bad grades don't automatically appear. If you've been watching weekly reports and grades on papers and tests, you should have some idea of how your child is doing.

Even if a child's report card isn't as good as you would like, look for something positive—a grade raised in math or a teacher's comments about how hard your child is working—and show you are as pleased with your child's success, as you are concerned with less successful efforts. If you ground your child because of a bad report card, or if you yell and scream and say the child is lazy or stupid, you're probably making the situation worse. Be positive. Start with something you can make a difference with.

14. Meet the "boss." Meet your child's teacher at the beginning of the term. Many parents feel uncomfortable about contacting their child's teacher, and even more anxious if the teacher calls to request a meeting. Such feelings may be related to the parent's own childhood, when the teacher may have been a strong authority figure who defined what was right or wrong, passed judgment, or was overly critical. Keep in mind that most teachers are people too. They often come to parent-teacher conferences with their own apprehensions and uncertainties about how they will be viewed by you, the child's parents. Understanding the perspective of the teacher will help to make your relationship productive and enjoyable.

15. Schedule a "business" meeting. Some parents believe that parent-teacher conferences occur for one of two reasons: their child is behaving badly, or their child is having serious problems keeping up with schoolwork. Conferences are held for these reasons, but they're not the only conditions under which conferences occur. Conferences may serve quite a variety of functions: to report on the child's progress, to compare the teacher's understanding of the child with that of the parents (when the teacher has noticed something in the child's behavior that could be of concern), and to ask parents for specific help (for example, when a child is having difficulties with schoolwork that may be related to the home environment).

Remember that teachers aren't the only ones who can schedule conferences. You can take the initiative too. If you have specific questions, or if you want to know generally how your child is doing, or if you think there's a problem, make an appointment with the teacher immediately. Call the school to set it up. Don't expect to get a teacher out of class to speak to you, but do expect that the teacher will get back to you within a reasonable period of time. If you don't hear from the teacher within two days, call again because messages have a way of going astray. If after your second call there is no return call, ask to speak with the assistant principal. If you speak a language different from that of the teacher, ask if the school will provide an interpreter.

16. Remind children of their progress. For children, last year seems like a lifetime away. Children have difficulty putting things in perspective. You can motivate them to continue their efforts by showing them just how far they have come. You might pull out some old book reports and show the difference in writing, grammar, and organization. Perhaps you have saved some artwork that looks primitive by your teenager's current standards. The goal is to show your children that they have made remarkable progress and can continue to do so.

17. Ask for help. It has already become a joke of the '90s that parents have to get their children to program the VCR. We laugh, but it's true that children have much to teach us. Even very young children can give us information we never knew. Encourage your children by asking for their help. Of course, you don't want to be condescending; children can sense quickly when you are patronizing them. But you might be reading an article on Russia and wonder out loud to your children what the future of that country will be. Since they may have been discussing that very thing in current events, they will be glad to tell you about it. Older children might be able to help you with your computer. Each child has something to contribute.

18. Help your children set goals. Goal setting is a critical key to success, not only in school but in life. If you keep yourself informed of what your children are doing in school, you will be able to encourage them to set goals. These can be both short term (to learn the spelling words) and long term (to master that difficult violin solo by the end of the year). It's important to sit down and talk about goals, making sure they are realistic and attainable but still challenging. Put the goals down in writing to make them seem more real. Set up a calendar or timetable by which progress can be measured. If there are logical steps on the way to the goal, write them down. For example, your child may be able to do part of the violin solo by the end of the month, the more difficult passages in two months, and that nearly impossible fingering by the end of the year. Once you have the goals established, be sure to keep track of them. Don't let your children write them down to placate you and then toss them in a drawer and forget about them.

19. Give rewards. Remember how excited your small children were when they got their first gold stars on a spelling test? You probably were just as excited, posting the paper on the refrigerator. No matter the age of your children, they need to feel their work is being acknowledged and rewarded. While not all rewards are tangible, children like to get something substantial and concrete. We adults may be satisfied with praise and a pat on the back; a child would prefer a hot fudge sundae! My friend Suzee's mother had a red carpet that she would roll out from the front door to Suzee's bedroom whenever her daughter did something wonderful at school. Suzee studied twice as hard as she normally would, hoping to get that red carpet treatment. She would get so excited over a perfect score on a test that she would call her mother from school so the red carpet would be waiting when she got home.

20. Help your children cope with stress. School can be a stressful experience. Today, children have a tough academic load, plus sports, social activities, and half a dozen other activities, all demanding their time and attention. You need to be aware of some of the warning signs of stress and take steps to deal with it. My book, *Stress in Children: How to*

Recognize, Avoid, and Overcome It, lists these signs in detail and gives suggestions for dealing with them. It's important to your children's well-being that they have good coping skills. Their academic success is also affected by their ability to prevent or deal with stress. If they let themselves be overwhelmed, they will view schoolwork only as a source of discomfort and unhappiness and not achieve the success we want for them.

21. Be aware of other resources. There may come a time when you want to get outside help for your children. Small children might need extra help with reading skills. Older teenagers may want tutoring to help them with the SAT college entrance exam. Find out, from the schools, from the paper, and from friends, what outside resources are available. Many public libraries have reading groups in which volunteers read to children or tutors do one-on-one sessions. These are often free. If a child needs special help because of a learning disability (such as dyslexia), the school can probably recommend a specialist. There's someone out there who can help, no matter what the problem.

22. Teach assertiveness skills. School is the primary social experience for students of all ages. We send our children to school as much to learn how to deal with other children as to learn reading, writing, and arithmetic. If we want them to be academically safe, to stay in school, to see it as a positive experience, they need social skills that enable them to deal confidently and competently with other children. How good are your children's assertiveness skills? Do your children know how to stand up for themselves unequivocally but politely? How much do you know about how your children handle themselves when being bullied by others? Talk with them about the best ways to handle each situation assertively rather than aggressively.

Your goal is to show your children that any situation, no matter how frightening or hopeless it may seem, is manageable. When they know that, they will feel much more safe and secure in their academic world.

Parents may need help in understanding what distinguishes assertiveness from aggression. Assertiveness skills enable us to assert our rights without using intimidation or being intimidated. There are times when we want to tell others how we're feeling, what we think is important, and what we are willing or not willing to do. We'll need to be able to do this in a way that is accepted by others and gets the point across effectively. It doesn't do any good to yell or make people guess what our needs are. Besides, they'll most likely guess wrong, our needs will go unmet, and we'll be disappointed because our expectations haven't met with success. It also doesn't do much good to hope that if we're nice to people they'll somehow know what it is we need and give it to us.

Do Your Children Feel Capable?

A good way to test your children's ability to stand their ground is to use the following questions, or similar ones, in probing their skills individually. Select a time when you are feeling especially close. Most parents do this while they are in the car, window shopping, or at some other time when they are at leisure and are not hurried, anxious, or rushed. Here are some questions to begin with; you may wish to modify them.

- "A girl student asks to cut in front of you in a line. You don't want to let her in. What do you say?"
- "A school bully wants to read the same book you are

reading and grabs it out of your hand. The teacher is nowhere in sight. What do you do?"

- "A boy asks to copy your answers to a test. You don't want him to. What do you say?"

- "The teacher asks the entire class to stay after school because someone was talking. You don't want to take the blame for something you know isn't your fault. What do you do?"

- "You are working on a report, and the teacher says to hand it in right now. You know she told you you had an hour, and it's only been 50 minutes. What do you do?"

- "Your teacher changes her mind and tells you a large homework assignment is due on Monday, not Tuesday. You had already made plans for the weekend and won't have any time to work on the assignment. What do you do?"

- "You're in the cafeteria line and one kid calls you a name. The other kids join in, and soon everyone is teasing you. How do you react?"

- "You don't understand a problem the teacher has just explained. What would you say in asking for help?"

- "You have two good friends, and they are fighting. The first comes to you saying nasty things about the other. The second asks you to go to the mall, but insists that the first friend can't come along. What do you do?"

Not every child is going to be a straight-A student. Some students will have to work as hard as they can just to get C's. Parents need to help their children feel capable academically regardless of their grades. It's this attitude of capability, more than IQ or opportunity, that determines your children's willingness to do other things. Those with an attitude of "I can do it!" are willing to go the extra mile. Because they have that attitude, they usually make it to the finish line. With an increased sense of competence, children expect to do well and actually do better. In turn, positive experiences build a child's self-confidence. Each success stimulates this child's efforts, who soon has a storehouse of positive reminders of being capable, a "can-do" person.

Most children will have some failures, perhaps missing nearly every question on a pop quiz or getting a bad grade on a science project they thought was top-notch. If they feel capable, they are able to shrug off the failure or, better yet, learn from their mistakes. They still view themselves as strong and able and figure the problem can be remedied. Academically safe children are able to distinguish between a failure that was their fault ("I just didn't study hard enough; I'll have to put in more time next time") and one that was not ("I had a headache"). They will be able to put failures behind and move on. They will feel secure enough, safe enough, to take the next academic risk.

Helping our children feel safe academically means they know we are pulling for them to do their best, applauding their school successes and understanding their failures. Their feeling of safety and security allows them to take the risks that let them make the most of their school experience.

12

Are You Helping Your Children Set Purposeful Goals?

Going to school for the sake of getting good grades is not a purposeful activity for children. It's not a big enough vision. Yet children whose lives feel purposeful—unlike children with no direction, who often turn to peer groups or alcohol or drugs for succor—are vibrant, optimistic, and have a zest for living. The difference? They work toward important, meaningful goals.

You can best help your children to develop a sense of purpose by encouraging them to think through the meaning they want their lives to have. Help your children to identify the values and standards that guide their existence, form their thoughts, build their behavior. Once those values are clearly expressed, the best way to begin living by them is to develop goals. A goal is a plan. It is a means to an end, not an end in itself. A goal is the tangible expression of the means to live out one's values. For example, if you strongly value education, your goal might be to finish college. If you value human life, your goal might be to avoid drugs and alcohol and other self-destructive behaviors.

Teaching Your Children to Set and Achieve Goals

Are your children goal-oriented? Whether a child is six or sixteen, you can help with the cycle of setting and achieving goals. You want to help your children choose goals that are meaningful enough to motivate them to carry them out. Here are some questions to ponder.

What are your children's strengths? What does each child do well? Remember, we're all different. Your son might be good at languages, while his best friend is a powerful athlete, and another friend finds math and science easy. Sometimes it takes awhile to delineate those areas, but they're there. The more things your children are exposed to (as long as they have some time to explore them), the better the chances of finding what they're really good at.

I suggest that parents read one book every two or three months to their child, regardless of age. Read the biographies of exemplary people. Note that these individuals were ordinary people who possessed character, values, and dedication to follow their goals, and that this, more than anything else, was their real strength. Point out that there was usually one particular turning point in these people's lives. For example, a ballerina might have been taken to *Swan Lake* by her parents when she was just a child and said, "That's it, that's what I want to be."

What captures the attention? A key to helping your children set goals is to center them (at least in the beginning) around what they're good at. What captures a child's attention? We all do better in those things that interest us.

In physical education class, your daughter might like volleyball band be good at it. But how good is she at baseball or square dancing? Have you ever been doing something and lost all track of time? Watch for those times when your child is so absorbed or involved in a project that nothing else seems to matter. When your son is looking for a book in the library, what does he pick up and read? What informational programs does he watch on television? What class does he really enjoy? What activities does he choose? When he feels completely absorbed in something, what is he doing? If you take the time to write these down and examine them, you'll have a better composite picture. Talk about these areas of interest. Is he aware of them? What are his thoughts for achieving purposeful goals in these areas?

What do your children feel strongly about? Ask each child for a list of "wants." At first you'll hear a lot of different ideas; help select two or three and then get specific. Turn them into a goal. This goal may be broad and general, like "I want a new bike" or "I want a car" or "I want to be a veterinarian." Help examine them from every aspect to see which ones are really important and which are not. Say, "Yes, you want to be on the soccer team this year, but you don't sound very convincing. How much do you want this? Why is it important to you? What are you doing to make sure you make the team?"

Remember that a child will work harder and with more enthusiasm toward goals that are important. If sports sound like an interest, read stories of athletes together, or visit athletes in your town, or subscribe to magazines that highlight the challenges of the "thrill of victory and the agony of defeat." Your children will discover that they have to practice two, three, or more hours a day, often giving up other interests because being the best at their sport is usually their number one goal. Achieving a goal requires intensity of purpose.

What opportunities do you make available? What *you* expect becomes an important part of your children's aspirations. Something as simple as taking your daughter to a college campus when she's in eighth or ninth grade sets in motion a dream of wanting to go to college. In many cases, it's this very campus you visited that becomes the dream. If she does go there, this campus becomes a hallmark for her studies, the career she chooses, maybe even the man she marries, and usually serves as the location where she will begin a first job and sometimes the city in which she will begin a family. What opportunities do you create for this child—with her in mind, and not just those activities that are the most convenient to you?

Key Areas for Goal Setting

Here are key areas that give meaning to our lives. Help your children talk about their goals in each of these areas, why the goal is important, what their plan is for working at it, and then help develop a way to achieve it. You'll find the time you spend communicating with your children about these goals can be very meaningful. Each of these nine key areas has its place of importance and meaning in a child's life. Helping your children commit to goals in each area helps them to have a balanced life as well as to determine what is of importance.

- Peace of mind
- Good personal relationships
- Learning and education
- Status and respect

- Leisure time
- Physical fitness
- Financial security
- Productive work

With these areas in mind, you're more prepared to guide a child in setting goals. Here are some guidelines for helping your children bring their goals to fruition.

Six Questions to Direct Goal Setting

1. Whose goal is it? A child who doesn't really want something will not make the commitment needed to accomplish it. Children should "own" their goals. If you're trying to convince them to set a goal you would like to see attained, you're going to have to help them see it as their own, or they won't be very motivated toward achieving it. If you want your daughter to be a good student, that's one thing. But if *she* wants to be a good student, that's another. She's likely to be a good student because that is her goal too. She has to have an inner fire, a drive that says, "It's important to *me*."

2. Is the goal attainable? Children have to believe they can meet a goal; it must be achievable. Note that it doesn't have to be easy. But there has to be a better than fifty-fifty chance of success. You don't want a goal that is self-defeating, one that is so difficult a child almost certainly will not achieve it. The goal must be one that the child personally believes can be achieved.

It also has to be a challenge. There's a saying that goes, "Most people don't aim too high and miss, they aim too low and hit!" The same is true for the child that sets goals that are yours, or are too easy. If your son's goal is to get at least a C on his paper and he knows he can do better, what's the challenge? If his goal is to do at least twenty sit-ups and he can already do nineteen with no problem, what's the challenge?

3. What makes the goal worth achieving? What are the benefits? Is it worth the time and effort? When your child's teacher is lecturing and says, "Now, this next material will not be on the test, but you should know it anyway," what does your daughter do? Does she pay as much attention as she normally would, or does she exchange a grin with her friends, sit back, and relax? She probably just kicks back. She doesn't take the material seriously, because she knows she won't be tested on it. She assumes there's little benefit to taking notes and paying attention.

When you are helping your children set goals and begin working toward them, take a few minutes to talk about what they're going to get out of it—the benefits. Try this first yourself. Suppose one of your goals is to be in better physical condition. How many benefits can you think of that will motivate you toward the effort it's going to take? You might feel better physically, develop better body strength, do more activities with greater ease; you will feel better emotionally, look better, maybe get more positive comments from others who have observed your new health; you'll gain more confidence, and so on. The more reasons you think of for achieving the goal, the stronger will be your desire. And the stronger the desire, the easier it is to reach your goal.

4. Is the goal in writing? Have your children write their goals down. Writing a goal down makes it clear, provides an organized plan of attack, and, when crossed off, keeps track of progress. There's another reason to write down a goal. You internalize it and commit to it by putting pencil to paper. If it's just in your head, you can easily forget about it. We have hundreds of thousands of thoughts daily; most are forgotten in moments. But those we take the time and effort to focus on matter more.

Suppose you want to build a house, and you hire an architect. He meets with you and says, "I have a lot of great ideas. Here I'm going to put the master bedroom with high ceilings; here I am going to put the Jacuzzi; here I'm going to put the living room."

You listen for a while, then say, "I'm having trouble remembering and visualizing all this. May I see your blueprints, please?"

The architect smiles at you. "Blueprints? I never write anything down. I keep it all in my head!" Are you going to let this person design your house? Probably not. Even if the architect is a genius, no one can work without a blueprint. The same is true for your children's goals. Writing them down provides a blueprint for their efforts. Then post the goals where they can see them. A child's vision can be pretty shortsighted. I talk with many children who set goals, but by the end of the week, they've lost sight of them. Make several copies and post them in conspicuous places: on the mirror, on the refrigerator, and on the child's notebook.

5. Are the deadlines realistic? Teach your children how to break long-term goals into short-term goals. For example, to reach the long-term goal of getting into college, break it down into a series of short-term goals, ranging from doing well in college prep classes to getting the money together for tuition.

Goals and deadlines seem a lot easier to reach when they are broken down into manageable tasks. Help your children set dates for each goal, major and minor. Some dates are predetermined, such as the SAT college admission exam. But one can still set intermediate deadlines: to have the vocabulary learned by this date, the math by that date, and so on. Having a date written down motivates us and helps manage the task. It also helps prioritize where and how we will allocate time. Then, when we see a deadline approach, we can push just a little harder or know when to plan down time and play time. When we do accomplish our goal within the deadline, we feel successful.

Make sure your children don't set overly ambitious deadlines. Don't let your son put down that he's going to make ten new friends this month if he's a very shy person who has trouble making two friends a year. Don't let your daughter record that she's going to take ten seconds off sprint time, if she hasn't taken off more than one second a semester so far. Don't set an A as the goal in math if the child is not even getting C's now.

6. Has a reward been established? Let's say that your daughter has set a goal and accomplished it. She did something she set her mind to do and deserves to be proud of herself and to take time to feel the satisfaction of having accomplished something purposeful. Teach her to do something nice for herself as a reward. Ask her, "What one nice thing will you do for yourself, because you have been diligent and hard at work on your goal?" Maybe it's just a few days of down time, or a new item of clothing, or tickets to a special concert. This is a form of praise best generated by your child for her accomplishments.

Young Children Need Goals

Even first-graders are not too young to learn how to set goals. I teach parents to use what is called a "wish list" to help children generate two or three things that are important to achieve. Take a piece of tag board, have your child draw a picture of each goal on the board, and hang it in your child's room as a constant reminder. Children's goals are large or small. They can be as important as developing a sense of responsibility by feeding and watering the family pet every day or as seemingly minor as keeping a room clean for two weeks. The importance of goal setting is to empower your children to look forward to what is of purpose—to what is worth spending time on. In the beginning, it serves as a way of helping children learn to be responsible.

You might be surprised at how diligently a young child is willing to work at achieving a goal—if it seems important. One small child I knew decided that her "leisure time" goal was to learn to ride her two-wheeler. She achieved her goal three days later, although before she verbalized it and wrote it down she hadn't seemed to be able to do so.

Today, many elementary schools invite children from kindergarten up to enter an annual science fair. Parents will probably never find more enthusiastic students for such science projects than their five- to seven-year-olds. If you suggest they might want to set their "learning and education" goal around that science fair, most young children will avidly comply. With a bit of investigating for those things they really want to learn about (an animal? the ocean? shells or rocks? stars? why leaves fall in autumn? how incense is made?—the possibilities are endless) you can watch your children wholeheartedly throw themselves into learning. Smaller goals, such as getting to the library and finding children's books on the subject, can be made and met along the way.

A young single mother I knew made a large night sky on a huge poster board then hung it in her children's bedroom. She asked her five- and three-year-old to do and remember one thing each day that would make God happy. Each of these small "spiritual goals" meant a star for the night-sky poster in their room. The child placed each star personally and worked on winning them. The point is not that the goals were impressive but that young children were learning to set and achieve them. The gratification of seeing their sky poster fill up and look prettier was a bonus to the real benefits: being aware of the good they had done and feeling good about themselves because of it.

While this single mother was not consciously having her children set goals, and I don't necessarily mean to suggest you should start your children setting goals this young, I still find value in her story. As we see, with younger children the goals may have to be modified to take less time to achieve, to allow for more concrete forms of progress being made, and perhaps to have more visible forms of their accomplishment. Still, with time and thought, this can be one of the most enjoyable exercises for nurturing self-esteem in a young child.

We all need to feel purposeful. The need to feel purposeful is even stronger in children, who often believe they have little control over their lives. They eat whatever food is served, go where they are taken by Mom and Dad, do what the teachers tell them to do. Feeling purposeful helps children feel like vital and worthwhile contributors to the family and to society.

Suggested Reading

Anderson, Eugene, George Tedman, and Charlotte Rogers. *Self-Esteem for Tots to Teens*. Deephaven, Minn.: Meadowbrook Press, 1984.

Baron, Jason D. *Kids and Drugs*. New York: G. P. Putnam's Sons, 1983.

Bedley, Gene. *The ABCD's of Discipline*. Irvine, Calif.: People-Wise Publications, 1979.

Bennett, William J. *Schools Without Drugs*. Washington, D.C.: U.S. Government Printing Office, 1989.

Bergstrom, Corinne. *Losing Your Best Friend*. New York: Human Sciences Press, 1980.

Berne, Eric. *What Do You Say After You Say Hello?* New York: Grove Press, 1971.

Berne, Patricia, and Louis Savary. *Building Self-Esteem in Children*. New York: Continuum Publishing Co., 1989.

Bessell, Harold, and Thomas Kelly, Jr. *The Parent Book.* Rolling
Hills Estates, Calif: Jalmar Press, 1977.

Betancourt, Jeanne. *Am I Normal?* New York: Avon Books, 1983.

Bingham, Mindy, et al. *Choices: A Teen Man's Journal for Self-
Awareness and Personal Planning.* El Toro, Calif.: Mission Publications, 1985.

————. *Choices: A Teen Woman's Journal for Self-Awareness and
Personal Planning.* El Toro, Calif.: Mission Publications, 1985.

Blume, Judy. *Are You There, God? It's Me, Margaret.* New York:
Dell Publishing Co., 1970.

Bonny, Helen L., and Louis Savary. *Music and Your Mind.* New
York: Harper & Row, 1973.

Booraem, Curtis, John Flowers, and Bernard Schwartz. *Help
Your Children Be Self-Confident.* Englewood Cliffs, N.J.:
Prentice-Hall, 1978.

Bradley, Buff. *Where Do I Belong? A Kid's Guide to Stepfamilies.*
Reading, Mass.: Addison-Wesley Publishing Co., 1982.

Branden, Nathaniel. *Psychology of Self-Esteem.* New York: Bantam
Books, 1969.

Briggs, Dorothy. *Celebrate Your Self.* Garden City, N. Y.: Doubleday & Co., 1977.

————. *Your Child's Self-Esteem.* Garden City, N.Y.: Doubleday &
Co. Dolphin Books, 1975.

Brookover, W. B. *Self-Concept of Ability and School Achievement.*
East Lansing, Mich: Office of Research and Public Information, Michigan State University, 1965.

Buscaglia, Leo. *Living, Loving and Learning.* Thorofare, N. J.: Charles B. Slack, 1982.

————. *Love.* Thorofare, N. J.: Charles B. Slack, 1972.

Cetron, Marvin J. *Schools of the Future.* New York: McGraw-Hill Book Co., 1985.

"Children Having Children: Teen Pregnancy in America." *Time,* December 9, 1985, pp. 78–90.

Clems, Harris, and Reynold Bean. *Self-Esteem: The Key to Your Child's Well-Being.* New York: G. P. Putnam's Sons, 1981.

Coopersmith, Stanley. *The Antecedents of Self-Esteem.* San Francisco, Calif.: W. H. Freeman & Co., 1967.

Covey, Stephen R. *The Seven Habits of Highly Effective People.* New York: Simon & Schuster, 1989.

Covington, M. V. "Self-Esteem and Failure in School," *The Social Importance of Self-Esteem.* Berkeley, Calif.: University of California Press, 1989.

Crockenberg, Susan, and Barbara Soby. "Self-Esteem and Teenage Pregnancy," *The Social Importance of Self-Esteem.* Berkeley, Calif.: University of California Press, 1989.

Crow, Lester D., and Alice Crow. *How to Study.* New York: Macmillan Publishing Co., Collier Books, 1980.

Davis, Lois, and Joel Davis. *How to Live Almost Happily with Your Teenagers.* Minneapolis: Winston Press, 1982.

Dobson, James. *Preparing for Adolescence.* Santa Ana, Calif.: Vision House, 1978.

Dodson, Fitzhugh. *How to Discipline with Love.* New York: Rawson Associates, 1977.

"Do You Know What Your Children Are Listening To?" *U.S. News & World Report*, October 28, 1985, pp. 17–26.

Dreikurs, Rudolf. *Children: The Challenge.* New York: Hawthorn Books, 1964.

Drew, Naomi. *Learning the Skills of Peacemaking.* Ed. Janet Lovelady. Rolling Hills Estates, Calif.: Jalmar Press, 1987.

Dyer, Wayne. *What Do You Really Want for Your Children?* New York: William Morrow & Co., 1985.

Elkind, David. *All Grown Up and No Place to Go: Teenagers in Crisis.* Reading, Mass.: Addison-Wesley Publishing Co., 1984.

"Family Fitness: A Complete Exercise Program for Ages Six to Sixty-Plus." *Reader's Digest* (Special Report), 1987, pp. 2–12.

Feingold, Norman S., and Nora Reno Miller. *Emerging Careers: New Occupations for the Year 2000 and Beyond.* Garrett Park, Md.: Garrett Park Press, 1989.

Fensterheim, Herbert, and Jean Baer. *Don't Say Yes When You Want to Say No.* New York: Dell Publishing Co., 1975.

Fox, Emmet. *Alter Your Life.* New York: Harper & Brothers, 1936.

————. *Power Through Constructive Thinking.* New York: Harper & Brothers, 1938.

————. *The Sermon on the Mount.* New York: Harper & Brothers, 1938.

Fromm, Erich. *The Art of Loving.* New York: Bantam Books, 1963.

Frost, Gerhard. *Homing in the Presence: Meditations for Daily Living.* New York: Harper & Row, 1978.

Gardner, Richard. *The Boys and Girls Book About Stepfamilies.* New York: Bantam Books, 1982.

Getzoff, Ann, and Carolyn McClenahan. *Stepkids: A Survival Guide for Teenagers in Stepfamilies.* New York: Walker & Co., 1984.

Harris, Thomas A. *I'm OK—You're OK.* New York: Avon Books, 1967.

"Has Rock Gone Too Far?" *People Magazine,* September 16, 1985, pp. 47–53.

Haynes-Klassen, Joanne. *Learning to Live, Learning to Love: A Book About You, a Book About Everyone.* Rolling Hills Estates, Calif.: Jalmar Press, 1985.

Hirshberg, Charles, and Denise Stinson. "Bayton's Boys Do the Right Thing." *Life Magazine,* September 1991, pp. 24–32.

Holly, William. "Self-Esteem: Does It Contribute to Students' Academic Success?" Eugene, Ore.: Oregon School Study Council, University of Oregon, 1987.

Holt, John. *How Children Learn.* New York: Delta Books, 1967.

Hyde, Margaret O. *Parents Divided, Parents Multiplied.* Louisville, Ky.: Westminster/John Knox Press, 1989.

James, Muriel, and Dorothy Jongeward. *Born to Win.* Menlo Park, Calif.: Addison-Wesley Publishing Co., 1971.

Jampolsky, Gerald G. *Teach Only Love: The Seven Principles of Attitudinal Healing.* New York: Bantam Books, 1983.

Kalb, Jonah, and David Viscott. *What Every Kid Should Know.* Boston: Houghton Mifflin Co., 1976.

"Kids and Cocaine: An Epidemic Strikes Middle America." *Newsweek*, March 17, 1986, pp. 58–63.

LeHaye, Tim. *The Battle for the Family.* Old Tappan, N.J.: Fleming H. Revell Co., 1982.

LeShan, Eda. *What's Going to Happen to Me? When Parents Separate or Divorce.* New York: Macmillan Co., Four Winds Press, 1978.

Maslow, Abraham. *Toward a Psychology of Being.* New York: D. Van Nostrand Co., 1962.

McCabe, Margaret E., and Jacqueline Rhoades. *How to Say What You Mean.* Willits, Calif.: ITA Publications, 1986.

McCullough, Christopher J., and Robert W. Mann. *Managing Your Anxiety: Regaining Control When You Feel Stressed, Helpless, and Alone.* Los Angeles: Jeremy P. Tarcher, 1985.

Miller, Gordon P. *Teaching Your Child to Make Decisions.* New York: Harper & Row, 1984.

Montessori, Maria. *The Discovery of the Child.* Notre Dame, Ind.: Fides Publishers, 1967.

Moses, Jeffrey. *Oneness: Great Principles Shared by All Religions,* New York: Fawcett Books, 1989.

Newman, Mildred, and Bernard Berkowitz. *How to Be Your Own Best Friend.* New York: Random House, 1973.

Palmer, Patricia. *Liking Myself.* San Luis Obispo, Calif.: Impact Publications, 1977.

Peale, Norman Vincent. *You Can If You Think You Can.* Pawling,

N.Y.: Foundation for Christian Living, 1974.

Pelletier, Kenneth R. *Mind as Healer, Mind as Slayer.* New York: Delacorte Press, 1977.

Postman, Neil. *The Disappearance of Childhood.* New York: Delacorte Press, 1982.

Richards, Arlene K., and Irene Willis. *Boy Friends, Girl Friends, Just Friends.* New York: Atheneum Publishers, 1979.

Samples, Bob. *Openmind-Wholemind: Parenting and Teaching Tomorrow's Children Today.* Rolling Hills Estates, Calif.: Jalmar Press, 1987.

Sanderson, Jim. *How to Raise Your Kids to Stand on Their Own Two Feet.* Chicago: Congdon & Weed, 1978.

Satir, Virginia M. *Peoplemaking.* Palo Alto, Calif.: Science & Behavior Books, 1972.

Sheehy, Gail. *Pathfinders.* New York: William Morrow & Co., 1981.

Sheinkin, David, et al. *Food, Mind, and Mood.* New York: Warner Books, 1980.

Silberstein, Warren P., and Lawrence Galton. *Helping Your Child Grow Slim.* New York: Simon & Schuster, 1982.

Skager, Rodney. *Prevention of Drug and Alcohol Abuse.* Sacramento, Calif.: California Attorney General's Office, 1988.

Skoglund, Elizabeth R. *To Anger with Love.* New York: Harper & Row, 1977.

Smith, Manuel J. *When I Say No, I Feel Guilty.* New York: Bantam Books, 1975.

Stainback, William, and Susan Stainback. *How to Help Your Child Succeed in School.* Deephaven, Minn.: Meadowbrook Press, 1988.

Steffenhagen, R. A., and Jeff D. Burns. *The Social Dynamics of Self-Esteem: Theory to Theory.* New York: Praeger Publishers, 1987.

"Teenage Fathers." *Psychology Today,* December 1985, pp. 66–70.

Unell, Barbara, and Jerry Wyckoff. *Discipline Without Shouting or Spanking: Practical Options for Parents of Preschoolers.* Deephaven, Minn.: Meadowbrook Press, 1988.

Viscott, David. *The Language of Feelings.* New York: Pocket Books, 1976.

Wahlroos, Sven. *Family Communication.* New York: Macmillan Publishing Co., 1974.

Warren, Neil C. *Make Anger Your Ally: Harnessing Our Most Baffling Emotion.* Garden City, N.Y.: Doubleday & Co., 1983.

Willing, Ken. *Perhaps the Second Most Important Book You Will Ever Read.* La Jolla, Calif.: Free Gift Press, 1984.

Winn, Marie. *Children Without Childhood.* New York: Pantheon Books, 1981.

Youngs, Bettie B. *Friendship Is Forever, Isn't It?* Rolling Hills Estates, Calif: Jalmar Press, 1990.

―――――. *Goal-Setting Skills for Young People.* 2nd ed. Rolling Hills Estates, Calif.: Jalmar Press, 1992.

―――――. *Helping Your Teenager Deal with Stress: A Parent's Guide to the Adolescent Years.* San Diego: Learning Tools, 1986.

―――――. *Problem Solving Skills for Children.* 2nd ed. Rolling Hills Estates, Calif.: Jalmar Press, 1991.

————. *Self-Esteem for Professional Educators: It's Criteria #1.* Rolling Hills Estates, Calif.: Jalmar Press, 1992.

————. *The Six Vital Ingredients of Self-Esteem and How to Develop Them in Your Child.* New York: Macmillan Co./Rawson Associates, 1991.

————. *Stress in Children: How to Recognize, Avoid, and Overcome It.* New York: Avon Books, 1985.

————. *A Stress Management Guide for Young People.* 2nd ed. Rolling Hills Estates, Calif.: Jalmar Press, 1992.

————. *You and Self-Esteem: A Book for Young People.* Rolling Hills Estates, Calif.: Jalmar Press, 1992.

How to Find Help

800 Numbers

ALCOHOL AND DRUG PROBLEMS

Alateen, Alanon: 1-800-356-9996 (New York, 1-800-245-4656)

Alcohol: 1-800-ALCOHOL (1-800-252-6465)

Cocaine: 1-800-COCAINE (1-800-262-2463)

Mothers Against Drunk Driving (MADD): 1-800-426-6233

National Council on Alcohol and Drug Dependency (NCADD): 1-800-NCA-CALL (1-800-622-2255)

National Federation of Parents for Drug-Free Youth: 1-800-554-KIDS (1-800-554-5437)

National Health Information Clearinghouse: 1-800-336-4797

National Institute on Drug Abuse (NIDA): 1-800-662-HELP (1-800-662-4357)

Child Abuse

Child Help USA: 1-800-4-A-CHILD (1-800-422-4453)

Crisis counseling: 1-800-421-6353 (California, 1-800-352-0386)

National Center for Missing and Exploited Children: 1-800-843-5678, to report information

National Runaway Switchboard: 1-800-621-4000

Parents Anonymous (PA): 1-800-421-0353 (California, 1-800-352-0386)

Other Problems

AIDS: 1-800-342-AIDS (1-800-342-2437); for deaf, 1-800-243-7889

Food addiction: 1-800-USA-0088 (1-800-872-0088)

Runaways: 1-800-231-6946 (Texas, 1-800-392-3352)

National Information Centers

National Self-Help Clearinghouse: 212-840-1259 (City University of New York Graduate Center, Room 1206A, 33 West 42nd Street, New York, NY 10036)

Self-Help Center: 312-328-0470 (1600 Dodge Avenue, Suite S-122, Evanston, IL 60201)

Self-Help Clearinghouse: 201-625-9565; for deaf, 201-625-9053 (Saint Clares-Riverside Medical Center, Danville, NJ 07834); ask for "The Self-Help Sourcebook," a national directory.

National Groups

ALCOHOL AND DRUG PROBLEMS

Alanon and Alateen: P.O. Box 182, New York, NY 10159 *

Alcoholics Anonymous (AA): P.O. Box 459, Grand Central Station, New York, NY 10017

Children of Alcoholics Foundation, Inc.: Box 4185 Grand Central Station, New York, NY 10163; 212-754-0656

Cocaine Anonymous: 3740 Overland Ave., Suite 8, Culver City, CA 90034; 213-839-1141. For meetings in your state, call 1-800-347-8998.

Cocanon (family support group): 310-859-2206 or 714-647-6698.

Families Anonymous, Inc.: P.O. Box 528, Van Nuys, CA 91408; 818-989-7841 or 1-800-736-9805

Mothers Against Drunk Driving (MADD): Hurst, TX; 817-268-6233

Narcotics Anonymous: Box 9999, Van Nuys, CA 91409; 818-780-3951

Nar-Anon (family support group): Box 2562, Palos Verdes Peninsula, CA 90274; 310-547-5800

National Association of Children of Alcoholics: 11426 Rockville Pike, No. 100, Rockville, MD 20852; 301-468-0985

National Clearinghouse for Alcohol and Drug Information (NCADI): Box 2345, Rockville, MD 20847; 301-468-2600 or 1-800-729-6686

---

* Telephone numbers not given here are listed under **800 Numbers**

National Federation of State High School Association Target Programs: 11724 N.W. Plaza Circle, Kansas City, MO 64195; 816-464-5400

National Institute on Drug Abuse (NIDA): P.O. Box 2305, Rockville, MD 20852; 301-468-2600

Students Against Driving Drunk (SADD): 200 Pleasant St., Box 800, Marlboro, MA 01752; 508-481-3568

DYSFUNCTIONAL FAMILIES

Adults Molested as Children United (AMACU): P.O. Box 952, San Jose, CA 95108; 408-280-5055

Big Brothers/Big Sisters of America: 230 North 13th Street, Philadelphia, PA 19107; 215-567-2748

Family Service of America (FSA): 11700 West Lake Park Drive, Milwaukee, WI 53224; 414-359-1040

National Center for Missing and Exploited Children: 1835 K Street NW, Suite 700, Washington, DC 20006; 202-634-9821

National Coalition Against Domestic Violence: 2401 Virginia Avenue NW, Suite 305, Washington, DC 20037; 202-293-8860

Stepfamily Association of America: 28 Allegheny Avenue, Suite 1037, Baltimore, MD 21204; 410-823-7570

EATING DISORDERS

American Anorexia/Bulimia Association, Inc.: 418 E. 76th St., New York, NY 10021; 212-734-1114

Anorexia Bulimia Care, Inc.: Box 213, Lincoln, MA 01773; 617-259-9767

National Anorexic Aid Society: 1925 E. Dublin-Grandville Road, Columbus, OH 43229; 614-436-1112

National Association of Anorexia Nervosa and Associated Disorders: P.O. Box 7, Highland Park, IL 60035; 708-831-3438

Overeaters Anonymous, Inc.: 383 Ban Ness Ave., No. 1601, Torrence, CA 90501; 310-618-8835. For information about chapters or meetings in your city, call 1-800-743-8703

State Offices

Alabama: Department of Mental Health, Montgomery; 205-271-9250

Alaska: Office of Alcoholism and Drug Abuse, Juneau; 907-586-6201

Arizona: Office of Community Behavioral Health, Department of Health Services, Phoenix; 602-255-1152

Arkansas: Office on Alcohol and Drug Abuse Prevention, Department of Human Services, Little Rock; 501-371-2603

California: Department of Alcohol and Drug Programs, Sacramento; 916-323-2087

Colorado: Alcohol and Drug Abuse, Department of Health, Denver; 303-331-8201

Connecticut: Alcohol and Drug Abuse Commission, Hartford; 203-566-7458

Delaware: Bureau of Alcoholism and Drug Abuse, New Castle; 302-421-6101

Florida: Alcohol, Drug Abuse, and Mental Health Program, Tallahassee; 904-488-0900

Georgia: Alcohol and Drug Abuse Services, Division of Mental Health, Atlanta; 404-894-4204

Hawaii: Alcohol and Drug Abuse Branch, Department of Health, Honolulu; 808-548-4280

Idaho: Bureau of Substance Abuse, Department of Health and Welfare, Boise; 208-334-5935

Illinois: Department of Alcoholism and Substance Abuse, Chicago; 312-917-3840

Indiana: Division of Addiction Services, Department of Mental Health, Indianapolis; 317-232-7816

Iowa: Department of Substance Abuse, Des Moines; 515-281-3641

Kansas: Social Rehabilitation Services, Alcohol and Drug Abuse Services, Topeka; 913-296-3925

Kentucky: Department for Mental Health, Substance Abuse Division, Frankfort; 502-564-2880

Louisiana: Office of Prevention and Recovery from Alcohol and Drug Abuse, Baton Rouge; 504-922-0725

Maine: Office of Alcoholism and Drug Abuse Prevention, Department of Human Services, Augusta; 207-289-2781

Maryland: Drug Abuse Administration, Baltimore; 301-225-6910

Massachusetts: Division of Alcoholism, Boston; 617-727-1960 Division of Drug Rehabilitation, Boston; 617-727-8614

Michigan: Office of Substance Abuse Services, Lansing; 517-335-8809

Minnesota: Chemical Dependency Program Division, Department of Human Services, St. Paul; 612-296-8574, 612-296-4611

Mississippi: Division of Alcohol and Drug Abuse, Department of Mental Health, Jackson; 601-359-1297

Missouri: Division of Alcohol and Drug Abuse, Jefferson City; 314-751-4942

Montana: Alcohol-Drug Abuse Division, Department of Institutions, Helena; 406-444-2827

Nebraska: Division of Alcoholism and Drug Abuse, Department of Public Institutions, Lincoln; 402-471-2851

Nevada: Bureau of Alcohol and Drug Abuse, Human Resources/Rehabilitations, Carson City; 702-885-4790

New Hampshire: Office of Alcohol and Drug Abuse Prevention, Concord; 603-271-4638

New Jersey: Division of Alcoholism, Trenton; 609-292-0729 drug treatment programs: 609-292-0728

New Mexico: Drug Abuse Bureau, Health and Environment Department, Santa Fe; 505-827-2589 or 2587

New York: Division of Alcoholism and Alcohol Abuse, Albany; 800-ALCALLS
Division of Substance Abuse Services, Albany; 800-522-5353

North Carolina: Carolina Department of Human Resources, Raleigh; 800-662-7030

North Dakota: Division of Alcoholism and Drug Abuse, Bismarck; 701-224-2769

Ohio: Bureau on Alcohol Abuse Recovery, Department of Mental Health, Columbus; 614-466-3445
Bureau of Drug Abuse, Columbus; 614-466-7893

Oklahoma: Reach Out Hotline, Department of Mental Health, Oklahoma City; 800-522-9054

Oregon: Office of Alcohol and Drug Abuse Programs, Salem; 503-378-2163

Pennsylvania: ENCORE, Office of Drug Abuse Programs, Harrisburg; 800-932-0912

Rhode Island: Division of Substance Abuse, Cranston; 401-464-2191

South Carolina: Commission on Alcohol and Drug Abuse, Columbia; 803-734-9520

South Dakota: Division of Alcohol and Drug Abuse, Pierre; 605-773-3123

Tennessee: Division of Alcohol and Drug Abuse, Department of Mental Health, Nashville; 615-741-4241, 615-741-1924

Texas: Commission on Alcoholism and Drug Abuse Prevention, Austin; 512-463-5510

Utah: Division of Alcoholism and Drugs, Salt Lake City; 801-533-6532

Vermont: Office of Alcohol and Drug Abuse Programs, Waterbury; 802-241-2170

Virginia: Prevention Information Services, Richmond; 804-786-1530
treatment programs: 804-786-3906

Washington: Bureau of Alcohol and Substance Abuse, Olympia; 206-753-5866

Washington, D.C.: Office of Health Planning and Development; 202-724-5637

West Virginia: Division of Alcoholism and Drug Abuse, Department of Health, Charleston; 304-348-2276

Wisconsin: Office of Alcohol and Other Drug Abuse, Madison; 608-266-2717

Wyoming: Division of Community Programs, Department of Health and Social Services, Cheyenne; 307-777-6493